RHODODENDRONS
CAMELLIAS & MAGNOLIAS
2019

A ROYAL HORTICULTURAL SOCIETY GROUP

SHARING THE BEST IN GARDENING

Published in 2019 by the Royal Horticultural Society,
80 Vincent Square, London SW1P 2PE

ISBN 978 1 907057 93 9

Designed for the RHS by SHARON CLUETT
Edited for the RHS by SIMON MAUGHAN

Editor for the Rhododendron,
Camellia and Magnolia Group
BARRY HASELTINE

Opinions expressed by the authors are not necessarily those of the Royal Horticultural
Society or the Rhododendron, Camellia and Magnolia Group

The Rhododendron, Camellia and Magnolia Group is a Charitable Incorporated
Organisation, Registered Number 1161254

Printed by Page Bros, Norfolk

COVER ILLUSTRATIONS

FRONT COVER: *Magnolia campbellii* (Cathryn Baldock: cathrynbaldockphotography.com)
BACK COVER (*LEFT*): *Rhododendron* 'Maurice Kupsch' (Neil Porteous)
BACK COVER (*RIGHT*): *Camellia* 'Augusto Leal de Gouveia Pinto' (George Hargreaves)

SHARING THE BEST IN GARDENING

CONTENTS

Chairman's Foreword

As announced in our November bulletin, I am delighted to welcome His Royal Highness, The Prince of Wales, as our first Patron. He has a growing interest in Rhododendrons and Magnolias, and he is personally involved in selecting and planting these in his gardens. His Patronage is a great honour and a welcome endorsement of our charity's aims and mission. I hope that our conservation projects in saving rare species and hybrids are closely matched with his own well-known views. Within this yearbook are some fascinating articles about our three genera, and I trust these will be educational and inspiring for The Prince of Wales, and all our membership too.

2019 marks the centenary of Lionel de Rothschild's epic garden creation at Exbury. Famously describing himself a 'banker by hobby but a gardener by profession' there can be few other gardens in the world created on this scale and with the fervour of one man, then to be passed on through the succeeding generations of his family. Now justly famous for its hybrid rhododendrons and azaleas, with more raised and registered than anywhere else, it is perhaps easy to forget that Lionel was an avid supporter of the great plant collectors, leading the syndicates that sponsored Forrest and Kingdon Ward to bring back plant gems from the Himalayas that had never been seen in the UK before. But what happened to all those wonderful species, as they seem to have been lost at Exbury and replaced by hybrids over the intervening years? No doubt they were used for breeding new varieties on an industrial scale, but now they are lost. I suppose this is partly due to the success of the breeding programme which bred better, stronger and showier plants, but the intervention of war, a mysterious fire which lost the gardener's records and drought on the sandy New Forest soil, all took their toll on the species collection.

This brings me to the ephemeral nature of all our gardens, and the continual need for conservation and repeated propagation of endangered plants so that we do not lose choice and important specimens. We cannot hope to keep the 33,000 registered rhododendrons all going, so we need to be selective and preserve those plants that we really do need to save for posterity. The few specialist nurseries will be unable to scratch the surface of plant conservation, so it will be up to individuals and organisations such as the RCMG to take the initiative and propagate those that need saving. In William Stanger's article about his year in New Zealand you will read about the NZRA scheme to ensure that rare plants are established in at least 3 gardens with a similar climate. I like the sound of this, and it's something we should endeavour to emulate. With a co-ordinated approach, local groups could arrange propagation amongst members, followed by distribution to secure gardens, where they can be managed for the future. Now here's another challenge for the Plant Committee; to repeat what they have achieved with the Pickard Magnolia collection, by aiming to propagate and conserve the plants raised by Amos Pickard within the prestigious Canterbury Cathedral gardens.

At the risk of repeating myself again, I really hope that members will choose to get more involved with the running of the Group, and hence gain more interest in the plants of our three genera. The Group is run by a Committee of members with no paid positions, and we rely on volunteers of all types to help in the smooth running of the charity. Barry Haseltine stepped forward at short notice to become Lead Editor of the Yearbook last year, and he needs special thanks for what he has achieved. However, we do need a volunteer to work with Barry, as he is not getting any younger. The sub-editors can check the horticultural content, but we need someone with organisational skills and a good command of English language to ensure that all articles are up to standard and ready for publication.

As announced at the last AGM, I intend to stand down at the AGM this year, so I expect this to be my last Foreword. It has been my pleasure to serve as your Chairman for 5 years, and to work with so many dedicated volunteers on the Committee, but now its time for someone else to take over the reins. Do please contact our Secretary if you can help the Group in any way.

Editorial

Last year I reported on the arrangements for producing the Yearbook and they seemed to work. We were all very pleased to hear that Members found it interesting and up to the Group's previous standards. The production this year has followed the same procedure and the Commissioning Editors have been hard at work collecting articles and editing them for me to use in the final book. Without their efforts, there would not be a Yearbook, so many thanks on behalf of all of us to Polly Cooke, John Marston, David Millais, Stephen Lyus and the authors.

Members will know that our Chairman, David Millais, and our Vice-Chairman, Ivor Stokes, are standing down at the AGM, so there will be a new team in place for the future. I have decided that I will offer to act as Yearbook Editor for another year, so as to give the new Chairman time to find a new Editor. Ideally, someone would be in place, to work with me, in the autumn of 2019, for the start of production of the 2020 Yearbook. Of course, at my age, I cannot make a promise that I will do the next Yearbook, but I can say that I will, if I am able to.

The Chairman has remarked in his Foreword on the Centenary of the creation of the wonderful garden at Exbury. I am delighted that Lionel de Rothschild has prepared a feature on the Garden, so you can read all about the start and the development of it over the 100 years. We are fortunate that the AGM will be there on 1st June, when we can appreciate the scale and beauty of the garden again.

The Group tour last year went to Northern Ireland, and there we saw the result of an amazing transformation of a rocky island in the Strangford Lough into a well wooded, packed, spring garden. I immediately suggested an article on its creation, and we have one by the owner of Mahee Garden, Paddy Mackie.

Gardens seem to be rather a feature of this Yearbook, as Ned Lomax has given us a detailed view of Penjerrick Garden and the legacy of Samuel Smith, a name probably not well known to members but who was responsible for much hybridisation.

We do not forget Camellias, and Stephen Lyus has given a detailed introduction into the Camellia Dictionary – a most elaborate work. Many of you will have suffered from Camellia Petal Blight in your gardens; work to try and beat it is reported by an International group of researchers.

Magnolias feature in an article on the magnolia collection of the J C Raulston Arboretum at North Carolina State University together with an entirely different article by William Guerterbock concerning *Magnolia globosa* 'White Ensign' and other magnolias in his garden in Dorset.

Rama Lopez-Rivera might make your hair stand on end with his description of a trek through Taiwan's mid-level mountains in search of two little-known populations of *Rhododendron pachysanthum* – crossing ravines on the suspended rails of on old railway line, no longer supported by the bridge on which they once rested!

William Stanger has travelled around New Zealand in search of the native flora and to gain experience of local gardens particularly in respect of large-leaved rhododendrons. William was part sponsored by the Group and he gives us a very detailed report on his year's work.

The picture is completed with an article on Occidentale Azaleas, and another on hardy hybrids, including a report from Miranda Gunn on the Group's collection of hardy hybrids at Ramster.

The usual features are to be found again this year, but welcoming Sharon McDonald who has taken over as RHS Rhododendron Registrar from Alan Leslie. We have added a new feature this year on the winners of four RHS individual awards, nominations for which are within the gift of the Group.

The Group has been running a photographic competition for several years, and there have been some excellent entries. For this coming year, we are seeking entries of portrait-style photographs, see the March Bulletin. As the Editor of the Yearbook, I often need portrait photographs as opposed to landscape ones.

The Editorial panel hopes that you enjoy the results of their work, and wishes you an enjoyable season of our genera.

Exbury Gardens 100 Years

My grandfather and namesake, Lionel de Rothschild, once described himself as "a banker by hobby but a gardener by profession". It is hard for me to comment on the first part of that description, though the interwar years were relatively quiet times for the family bank, N M Rothschild & Sons, but there is no doubt that in everything concerning his garden he approached it with the utmost professionalism and that gardening – and horticulture generally – were his true life's work. I once did a casual count of the files of his private correspondence held at The Rothschild Archive in the City; the vast majority – maybe 90% – concerned gardening. His father had two fine gardens, at Ascott in Buckinghamshire and at Gunnersbury outside London, and Lionel was particularly influenced by James Hudson, head gardener at Gunnersbury Park and the first man to have achieved full marks in the RHS exams; Hudson in turn was influenced by William Robinson.

Lionel moved to the area in 1912 on his marriage to my grandmother, Marie-Louise Beer, but at first settled at Inchmery, some 2 miles south-east of Exbury; it is said that he could not get permission to close or move the road that ran behind the house – to alter the approach to the house – because it had a post box on it. In any event, the Great War intervened and Lionel, to his eternal sadness, was forbidden to join up by no less an authority than the King: the generation before in the family bank were all elderly and indeed all died in the war years; his brothers both served and one, Evelyn, was killed in Palestine. It is hard at this distance to indulge in psychoanalytic speculation but I do wonder

LIONEL DE ROTHSCHILD 1882–1942

whether he suffered from "survivor's guilt" and retreated into himself and his one true passion, gardening. Certainly my grandmother remembered him as being at his most relaxed with what he called his "gardening godfathers", the Cornish cousins J C and P D Williams, and the great expert W J Bean. She in turn only truly flourished out of his shadow, keeping his legacy alive after he died all too prematurely aged only 60 in 1942.

All that, however, lay in the future when, in 1919, he completed the purchase of Exbury and set about creating his garden. I do not believe he had a master plan; rather, the garden grew organically, expanding to fill the adjoining woods and incorporate existing ponds and features.

Each pond was dredged, enlarged and lined in concrete; rills were created between them. An old gravel pit eventually became one of the largest rock gardens in Europe: it was not immediately successful due to honey fungus and waterlogging and Lionel concluded wryly, "gardening would be too easy if it was always a success". Even before he started work in the garden, the ground was double-dug and spent hops introduced – the abiding mnemonic smell for those that did the digging. He was determined to work with the landscape, improving as he went but not altering the fundamental lay of the land. Every care was taken to make rhododendrons, his favourite plant – and ours – not only look at home but to feel at home too. Why rhododendrons? This readership may find this a foolish question but it deserves an answer and I feel there are several. First, this plant along with camellias and magnolias, and acers in the autumn, decorated the oak woodland in the way he desired, achieving the effect he wanted. Secondly, rhododendrons had become fashionable again:

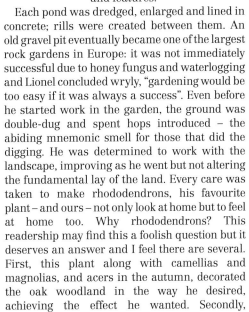

RHODODENDRON 'FRED WYNIATT' (*TOP*)
RHODODENDRON 'JESSICA DE ROTHSCHILD' (*BOTTOM*)
EXBURY GARDENS

THE TOP POND

EXBURY GARDENS

at the end of the 19ᵗʰ century it seemed as if not much remained to be discovered, though Hooker correctly forecast the amazing riches that lay in China; at the beginning of the 20ᵗʰ century it seemed these riches would never stop. In the second decade alone some 312 new species were added, more than the entire number described up to 1900. Thirdly, rhododendrons with their enormous variety of size and colour appealed to those two genes so prominent in my family, the collecting gene and the hybridisation gene. My cousin Miriam – herself a scientist – proposed this and while I am not entirely convinced, thinking such pursuits as much the product of wealth as of innate nature, there is no denying the extraordinary extent to which members of my family pursued their passions of amassing art or stamps, autographs or têtes de mort, and breeding animals or flowers. It should also be added that these are not genes in the true sense but rather traits and it is highly debatable whether they are inherited, acquired, learnt or all three.

Given the range of rhododendrons, Lionel could and did pursue many aims. One was to extend the season by breeding rhododendrons that flowered earlier and later. He liked clear reds, pastel pinks, orange bells and the flash of yellow. He wished to improve the hardiness by repeatedly "breeding in". He was adamant that the choice of parent was vital and he approached the whole thing a bit like his father had with racehorses. He used the pollen from the *R. sinogrande* at Trewithen to put on his *R. falconeri* because he considered it the best form: the result was the extraordinary *R.* 'Fortune'.

RHODODENDRON 'FORTUNE'

EXBURY GARDENS

RHODODENDRON CARITA GROUP   **EXBURY GARDENS**

RHODODENDRON 'CREST'   **EXBURY GARDENS**

My grandmother recalled him gathering the family round to show them and said the outstretched leaves reminded her of the Greek statue of Discobolus, ready for the throw. This was my father's favourite and for his ninetieth birthday I arranged for a bench to be put round a tree nearby and inscribed it to him with a suitable play on words: "It was his good fortune to inherit these gardens / It was their good fortune to inherit him".

In the case of my favourites, the *R. cinnabarinum* hybrids *R.* 'Lady Chamberlain', *R.* 'Lady Rosebery' and *R.* 'Lady Berry', he used forms of J C Williams's *R.* 'Royal Flush' as the pollen parent. One version of their genesis has Lionel snatching J C's crosses after the show, motoring straight down and making the crosses after dark! (In fact it appears J C Williams sent him the plants but it is characteristic of the myths that arose about him.) Another favourite of mine is *R.* 'Carita' and there is an unnamed creamy white form that, if it is good enough, I just might take for myself, *R.* 'Carita Lionel'. I never had anything named after me because of the confusion of names with my grandfather, whereas my twin sister Charlotte has a simply wonderful plant!

In the case of *R.* 'Hawk' and 'Crest' he made the same cross twice, using a different form of *R. wardii* as pollen parent the second time; he did not live to see the better version, which first flowered in the early 1950s. All in all he made 1210 crosses, of which some 462 were named; at a rough count this is a staggering 25% of inter-war hybrids. My father made some more crosses, but fewer than 200 crosses have been made since Lionel's day and none recently. I think one of the best is *R.* 'Jessica de Rothschild' (*R.* 'Hotei' × *R. decorum*), a most attractive flower. I keep saying I shall start and am drawn to try with lepidotes, especially retrying with cinnabarinums and maddenia. How wonderful it would be to have hardier equivalents to *R.* 'Lady Chamberlain' and less prone to powdery mildew!

RHODODENDRON 'CHARLOTTE DE ROTHSCHILD'   **EXBURY GARDENS**

In terms of collecting, Lionel helped fund all the famous plant collectors of the day, especially Farrer, Forrest and Kingdon-Ward. He arranged for Forrest's burial at Tengyueh and the return and distribution of the seeds. Kingdon-Ward's well-known affinity for the colour yellow – not that he ignored the others – paid handsome dividends. Kingdon-Ward visited often, even, according to my grandmother, when he really should not have: apparently he was at lunch and rather silent. "Kingdon-Ward, you look unhappy: are you alright?" she asked. "Yes, thank you Mrs Lionel. I just got married." "That is wonderful news. When?" "Today." "Today? What are you doing here then? You should be with your bride." "Mr Lionel asked me to lunch." "Lionel," she called, "Kingdon-Ward has just got married. Send for the Rolls-Royce." And off he went. This story illustrates the awe in which Lionel was held; in 1923 Kingdon-Ward wrote to Wright Smith, Keeper of the Royal Botanic Garden Edinburgh, about his recent visit to Exbury, "Within five years it will be the eighth wonder of the world."

Lionel was not content with having every rhododendron in existence – except *R. afghanicum*, as he wrote to Euan Cox, because of its extreme toxicity – but wished to place them to maximum effect. If either they were not happy or he felt they looked wrong, he would simply move them – their "little walks" – and only a few, which he duly he noted, would not respond. Evergreen azaleas were good as foreground against rhododendrons that had already flowered; purple clashed with red or pink (*R. niveum* was best on its own, for example); sealing-wax red did not go with crimson; white was good for separating other colours; magenta, that pre-eminent colour of the older Victorian hybrids, was either best on its own or eschewed entirely. Gardening is an art form in four dimensions, the fourth of which is time. One contemporary compared Lionel's garden to the herbaceous borders of Philip Sassoon (a distant cousin, as it happened): "Both of them had unlimited money at their disposal, both also had the most discerning eyes for colour and effect, and both were past masters in that most necessary of the arts of life, the art of anticipation ... Both could feel by instinct the effect of their designs."

There is no doubt that the garden we enjoy today is still his by design, its limits and lineaments discernibly his. Yet of course much time has passed: some plants are now at maturity; others have inevitably died. My grandmother kept it going during the war with a handful of elderly gardeners but much inevitably became overgrown. A bomb hit the rhododendron shed but there was little other damage; the worst was the grubbing up for farmland of his arboretum after the war. This lay across the road from the garden and was to hold every plant and shrub that could grow in the British Isles, advised upon, inevitably, by W J Bean

THE ARBORETUM AS PHOTO-GRAPHED BY THE LUFTWAFFE

EXBURY GARDENS

Approximate Scale 1:10,560 or about 6 inches to 1 mile

THE ROCK GARDEN

EXBURY GARDENS

himself. With characteristic directness, holes were made for planting by blasting with dynamite. The only surviving record is this reconnaissance photograph taken by the Luftwaffe. The navy occupied the house till 1955; when they left, my father first opened the garden to the public.

My father's taste is best described as kaleidoscopic: remembering now his taste in ties and jackets (if unchecked by my mother), I think his mantra was clearly "anything goes". To be fair, there was neither the unlimited money – my grandfather's death duties and debts had seen to that – nor the unlimited stock; when the Rock Garden was first cleared and brought back in the late seventies, I remember a preponderance of purple from what we had in stock.

Furthermore, my father entrusted much of the actual planting to the then head gardeners, Fred Wynniatt and then Douggie Betteridge. He was immensely proud of what they did and latterly, at his spring lunch parties held in a marquee, would always get poor Douggie – to his intense embarrassment – to stand up to take the applause. My father also loved doing the gardening himself, mainly brashing out dead wood or clearing brambles, and visitors would be surprised to hear a disembodied voice emerging from a dense bush: "Are you lost?"

My grandfather's first head gardener was Fred Kneller, who had been at Gunnersbury, and then Arthur Bedford. In those days Lionel organised the most stupendous exhibits at Chelsea. There was considerable rivalry between the grand gardens of the period, though it was always a friendly rivalry too, with much admiring of other people's exhibits. One time a sudden frost damaged many of the exhibits in the tent the night before: a quick telephone call to Exbury and fifteen lorries were dispatched at 4 am to mount a "staggering" display. Bedford returned from one of these shows a few years later, sat down on a bench, said, "Ah well, another Chelsea over" and died on the spot of a sudden thrombosis.

RHODODENDRON
YAKUSHIMANUM

EXBURY
GARDENS

However, his last words were also said to have been, "This field is full of daisies." Perhaps he said both. Bedford was succeeded by Francis Hanger, who went to Wisley after the war. Hanger it was who took one of the *R. yakushimanum* plants, later named as the Koichiro Wada form, while we retained the other, Exbury form (Koichiro Wada sent two plants in 1933 and another 1938 but by 1945 one had died). As we know, this has been named "Plant of the Century" in a recent poll of RCMG members.

After Hanger, Harold Comber took over but he clashed with my grandmother: she wanted to maintain Lionel's legacy; he wanted to take the garden in other directions. After them, Wynniatt and Betteridge, as mentioned, then Paul Martin who sadly died young, then Rachel Martin (no relation – for a while we had three or four people at Exbury, all unrelated and called Martin), then John Anderson (now at Savill Garden and Windsor) and now Tom Clarke. I list them all because while the family involvement has always been huge – and with my niece Marie-Louise Agius we are now on our fourth generation – there is no doubt that Exbury is the work of many hands.

Marie-Louise, a landscape gardener by profession, has designed a garden in a derelict tennis court that will be our Centenary Garden. This has been aimed primarily at herbaceous and summer flowering plants, with two fine *Heptacodium miconioides* at the end flanking a curved wooden bench, overlooking a sunken area in stone which is set with the five arrows from the family coat of arms. Around this are sash bars from an old greenhouse with wires supporting climbing roses. In four beds surrounding the sunken area are fastigiate ginkgos and herbaceous plants and grasses. This garden to some extent mirrors the adjoining Sundial Garden, which has a stone sundial in its centre and a beautiful stone gazebo trailing wisteria at one end. The Iris Garden has also been restored

MAGNOLIA INSIGNIS   EXBURY GARDENS

THE EXBURY GARDENS RAILWAY TRAIN

EXBURY GARDENS

for this coming year and will prove a fine addition to our summer features. One of the challenges at Exbury has been to attract visitors in times of year when the rhododendrons and azaleas are not in full bloom. As well as the items already mentioned, there are fine herbaceous beds near the house, a hydrangea walk and considerable planting for autumn colour. In addition to the Old and New Camellia Walks in the Winter Garden there is a new Camellia area, the Gilbury Lane Garden, which includes plants chosen and given by Jennifer Trehane. We have been steadily adding to our collection of magnolias: readers will be familiar with the fine *M.* × *veitchii* 'Peter Veitch' by Gilbury Bridge, the *M. campbellii* in the Home Wood and the iconic huge trees of *M. insignis* (formerly *manglietia*), introduced here in 1919, but many have been added over the years, down the new Camellia Walk and elsewhere.

I am particularly fond of some of the newer yellow varieties and welcome suggestions for them and indeed for other magnolias too. Finally, we are developing the right habitat to attract dragonflies at one of our ponds, now appropriately renamed Dragonfly Pond, to add summer interest and help educate and enthuse younger visitors.

The Dragonfly Pond is on the route of the railway that was first installed by my uncle Leo in time for his 75th birthday in 2002. It runs a mile and a half, first through a garden specially created for it in an old quarry and then enters the main garden, skirting the Rock Garden, past the Domesday Yew (old but not that old!) and on through the American Garden, where newer American hybrids are planted. The engines and rolling stock are in the family racing colours of blue and gold and the track is 12¼" gauge. The engines are named after my grandmother and two aunts, with a diesel named after my father, and the carriages are named after various women in the family. Each coach takes about 15 people and the ride lasts about 20 minutes. My uncle liked nothing better than to dress up in his Exbury Gardens Railway outfit (boiler suit, cap etc.) and drive the train; HM The Queen visited and rode with him twice and other members of the royal family, including our Patron, HRH The Prince of Wales, have been on it. My uncle's other great passion was classical music and he sang in

THE AUTHOR AND
HIS DOGS

EXBURY GARDENS

the Bach Choir – and was eventually its chairman – for over 50 years. Our Patron is Patron of the Bach Choir too and there is a particularly fine rhododendron, *R. fortunei* × Jalisco Group, named *R.* 'Bach Choir'.

My grandfather had a clear idea of what he wanted and achieved a truly remarkable amount in a short time. My father wanted to preserve that legacy while bringing back areas that had fallen into disrepair in the war and replacing plantings as they inevitably matured or after the two great storms. We now operate more by committee. Many day-to-day decisions are made by Tom Clarke but after our board meetings there are always walks round and, sometimes, selected decisions to be made. Largely we seem to agree, to my surprise! I do not see the essential woodland garden nature of Exbury changing in the short term, though I acknowledge that climate change poses serious challenges. My grandfather lamented the lack of water and our average of 25in of rainfall is pitiful for such thirsty plants; furthermore, in recent years we have had drier summers and wetter winters. Add to this new and old pests and diseases and the overarching challenge of attracting enough visitors and you might think I have sleepless nights. Nothing, however, is more relaxing and rewarding than a spring evening walk with my beloved dogs (vizslas, in case you were curious) through a garden filled with the plants honoured by this group – rhododendrons, camellias and magnolias.

RHODODENDRON 'BACH CHOIR'   EXBURY GARDENS

LIONEL DE ROTHSCHILD
is the grandson of the founder of Exbury Gardens, which celebrates its centenary this year. He has written on 19th century hybrids for The Rhododendron Story and has co-authored and co-photographed the book The Rothschild Gardens with his late cousin Miriam. He is actively involved at Exbury as well as in the family archive in London

Rhododendron occidentale and its modern-day plant hunters

RHODODENDRON OCCIDENTALE growing by Hunting Creek, California
MOLLY NILSSON

Rhododendron occidentale is a species deciduous azalea from the USA. Since this species was discovered, its value as a parent in hybridisation programmes in Europe and particularly in the UK, was recognised almost immediately. However, it wasn't until the 1950s that American plantsmen became really fascinated by *R. occidentale*. Since then, interest has grown apace and today there are numerous plant hunters and groups of enthusiasts that trek, every year, through the rugged terrain that is home to *R. occidentale*. Their objective is to find new intraspecific variants and to renew their acquaintance with old friends, both human and plant.

This article will tell you a little about *R. occidentale* growing in the wild and its habitat, the photos will say more than any words can; there are short biographies of some of the most notable Plant Hunters of recent times. They have brought wonderful selections of this species to our attention. Some of them have also found amazing mutations of *R. occidentale*. I touch on propagation, hybrids and where you can see these fascinating plants in the USA but I leave the detailed taxonomy to the experts.

RHODODENDRON OCCIDENTALE (Palomar 1318)
MIKE MCCULLOUGH

R.OCCIDENTALE AND *R. MACROPHYLLUM* growing at Lone Mountain "Ghost" Forest after a wildfire **DICK CAVENDER**

RHODODENDRON OCCIDENTALE:
ITS HABITAT AND ITS HISTORY

The Western Azalea, *Rhododendron occidentale*, is an isolated species native only to California and South West Oregon, in the far west of the USA. This deciduous shrub adorns many stream sides, emitting its marvellous sweet, musky fragrance on warm June and July days. It is found from sea level to over 2700m. The basic habitat of *R. occidentale* is on soils formed from specific rock types but always where there is sufficient water. From the northern end of its range near Myrtle Creek, Oregon, to roughly the latitude of San Francisco in the south, this soil type is ultramafic or serpentine; south of this, *R. occidentale* is found on soils derived from other mafic rocks but always near water.

N.B. Serpentinite is a metamorphic rock that is largely composed of Serpentine Group Minerals e.g. antigorite, lizardite and chrysotile. These hydrous silicate minerals, rich in magnesium, are called serpentine minerals, as they resemble a snake's skin. Antigorite is green in colour as much of the magnesium has been replaced by iron. All are poor in calcium. Care must be taken in handling soils containing chrysotile, the fibrous form of serpentine rock, as it is a source of asbestos. Mafic rock (ma from magnesium and fic is the latin word for iron) has a high content of both magnesium and ferric oxides.

R. occidentale and *R. macrophyllum* are known as 'Pioneer Species' as they both thrive after a wildfire. The Biscuit fire area in the Siskiyou National Forest is a perfect example; the fire covered about 500,000 acres, mostly in Oregon, burning from late July until December in 2002. Dick Cavender, a modern day plant hunter, visited a serpentine area west of Cave Junction, Oregon, in 2005. The forest on serpentine rock there was sparse, consisting of very stunted pines but both *R. occidentale* and *R. macrophyllum* were 3ft tall and flowering. He has witnessed this again in 2011 at Lone Mountain Forest and at Chrome Ridge in 2018.

LEAVES OF *R.* 'WASHINGTON STATE CENTENNIAL'   HAROLD GREER

R. occidentale was first discovered during the British expedition of Captain Beechy in 1827 and was also collected later by Douglas, Hartweg and Burke. At first it was not recognised as a distinct species being named in 1855 by Torrey and Gray as Azalea californica; a year later this was changed to Azalea occidentale. *R. occidentale* was introduced into cultivation by William Lobb, who sent seeds from California in about 1850 to the Veitch Nursery in Exeter; a plant from these seeds flowered in 1857. Anthony Waterer Senior of Knap Hill Nursery was the first known hybridizer of *R. occidentale* in the 1860's. He apparently had a poor success rate for nearly ten years. It is thought that he probably used *R. occidentale* as the pollen parent at first, and later had flower-producing plants to use for seed parents. His hybridisation of the Ghent azaleas with *R. occidentale* was the beginning of the Knap Hill azaleas. There is a very large plant of *R. occidentale* growing at the former Knap Hill Nursery in Surrey, believed to date from the 1860's. The Dutch Nursery, Koster's, also produced deciduous azalea hybrids using *R. occidentale* from about 1895. Later the Exbury hybrid deciduous azaleas were developed by the Rothschilds using *R. occidentale* as a parent.

R. occidentale is a diploid with the exception of Double Dig 12 which is a tetraploid. In 1972, Frank Mossman wrote the following concerning his hybridization with *R. occidentale*, a diploid: "We have found that *Rhododendron occidentale* will cross with many other rhododendrons or azaleas if *R. occidentale* is the seed parent, but *R. occidentale* as a pollen parent produces few seed." [1]

R. occidentale is a very variable species which is what makes it so fascinating. It is a totally isolated species, producing an enormous variety of flower size and colour, most but not all having the characteristic yellow blotch. The truss size too is variable, with anything from the average 5–12 flowers per truss, up to 25–54 flowers per truss in selected forms. *R. occidentale* is a much-branched sturdy shrub growing up to about 4.5 m tall. The variability within the species makes definitive morphology more complex than this article can cover. Suffice to say that the degree of pubescence seems to be a function of the availability of water. The leaf shape and size is equally variable but one thing is certain, the leaves change from green to yellow, crimson or scarlet in the autumn.

MODERN DAY *R. OCCIDENTALE* PLANT HUNTERS

Leonard Frisbie, a nurseryman based in Tacoma, Washington was a breeder of *Rhododendron occidentale* hybrids in the 1950s. He was a devotee of the genus, collecting his own material in the wild. Dr Edward Breakey was President of the Tacoma Rhododendron Society. Between them a study of *R. occidentale* began which led to a number of publications in the USA. Dr Breakey co-authored an article on *Rhododendron occidentale* with Leonard Frisbie in the 1955 Rhododendron and Camellia Yearbook.

Leonard wrote in 1967, "My first field trip was to South West Oregon, Curry County, and the experience was more of an emotional shock than anything else. Intellectually it was a blank. There were so many azaleas, all crowded into thickets,

R. OCCIDENTALE SM232 'LEONARD FRISBIE' A wild selected form registered by Smith and Mossman in 1971
TIM WALSH

millions of fragrant flowers. Nothing in my former experiences had prepared me for this. It was a bit frustrating to an inexperienced plant collector who had ambitions to accomplish something definite. But it was an essential beginning, and it had to happen in just about that way. It taught me that I knew little, valuable information this when one faces a big task, and I was convinced that my *R. occidentale* survey was going to be neither easy nor short. I also realized that if I were to learn about the azalea I would need to pursue it intellectually, not emotionally"[2].

Their work inspired others to take an avid interest in *R. occidentale*:

Britt Smith and Frank Mossman developed an intense passion for *R. occidentale*, making many

trips in the 1960s to the wild for 15 years or more. Dr Frank Mossman, who's significant work with azaleas and rhododendrons spanned several decades, passed away on November 2 2009. He was a doctor of Ophthalmology from Omaha, Nebraska. After his discharge from the army in 1945 his employment options were limited, with many doctors returning from the military. Luckily he secured a residency in Portland, Oregon where he worked for eight years before setting up a private practice in Vancouver, Washington.

During the first years in Portland, he developed his interest in rhododendrons, and started growing and propagating them. Britt Smith spent most of his career with the Boeing Company. Over the years Britt and Frank visited *R. occidentale* in the wild many times; one of the areas that they found the most unusual forms was on Stagecoach Hill, California. Their selection and registration of 'Humboldt Picotee' is a great example of a form of *R. occidentale* found there.

R. OCCIDENTALE SM502 'HUMBOLDT PICOTEE'   **KEN COX**

R. OCCIDENTALE 'FRANK MOSSMAN'   **DICK CAVENDER**

Early in their search for *R. occidentale*, Frank Mossman and Britt Smith met Jimmy Smith and his wife, who had a small nursery in Brookings, Oregon. There were plants of *R. occidentale* growing all around the area and Jimmy was quite interested in them. One of his acquaintances was a logger who told him of a *R. occidentale* growing at the edge of a forested area, bearing flowers which were completely yellow. The logger would neither bring Jimmy a truss nor tell him exactly where that plant was growing. Not long after that Jimmy moved house and they lost touch with him and also the link to that plant.

Frank chaired a National Convention in Portland in the early 1970s where one of the guest speakers was H. H. Davidian, from Edinburgh. Dr Davidian believed the observed large variation in *R. occidentale* flowers was due to interspecific and not intraspecific variation. When Frank took him on a trip to the occidentale habitats, he managed to convince Davidian that it was indeed intraspecific variation that produced the large floral variation.

R. 'TATUM'S DEEP PINK'   DICK CAVENDER

R. OCCIDENTALE SM042   BOB DUNNING*

The Smith/Mossman numbering system works as follows: Designations SM1, SM2, etc, were assigned to species plants as they were found during the first year of exploration. The second year designations SM101, 102, etc, were assigned in the order which they were found. In the third year, SM201, SM202, SM203, etc, so in the sixth year numbers SM501, SM502, SM503, etc were assigned.

The detailed and carefully kept notes from the expeditions of Smith and Mossman are much admired and are a treasury of information. In fact they can still be used today to locate plants of *R. occidentale* with the SM reference number.

Tom Tatum was a real plantsman and an expert on mushrooms. He was on call with hospitals in his area to make identifications in mushroom poisoning cases. He was a good friend of both Dick Cavender and Frank

Mossman; the three of them made several 'occidentale hunting' trips together. As far as we know, Tom was the first person to successfully grow Vireyas in North America. Dick Cavender registered two of Tom's occidentale collection, 'Tatum's Yellow Standard' and 'Tatum's Deep Pink' both of which were found by Tom in the Stagecoach Hill Azalea Reserve in the early 1970s. The latter was for many years one of the best pink-flowered *R. occidentale*. 'Tatum's Yellow Standard' is now extinct in the wild.

R. 'TATUM'S YELLOW STANDARD'   DICK CAVENDER

Eugene R. German (known as Gene German) was a member of the Noyo Chapter of the American Rhododendron Society, which meets in Fort Bragg, California. In the 1970s and in the 1980s, on a Saturday, about a week or two before the plant hunting expeditions of Britt Smith and Frank Mossman, Gene German would organize *R. occidentale* plant hunting expeditions. After

R. OCCIDENTALE GG1 at Flynn Creek   **MIKE MCCULLOUGH**

R. OCCIDENTALE (Idyllwild 1321)   **MIKE MCCULLOUGH**

meeting in Fort Bragg, they travelled east on Comptche Ukiah Road and then in a southerly direction on Flynn Creek Road.

On property owned by a lumber company, Gene German and companions would explore the *R. occidentale* in the upper reaches of the Albion River. Continuing in a southerly direction on Flynn Creek Road they would hike across the road and then down the gully to Flynn Creek. On the other side of the creek is *R. occidentale* GG1. All of Gene's discoveries are numbered and pre-fixed GG.

Carl A Deul from Northridge, California discovered a heat tolerant form of *R. occidentale*. There is a form of *R. occidentale* which grows in the San Jacinto Mountains near Idyllwild, California, which seems to be much tougher than the forms growing in the coastal areas of Northern California. Several people in the East and South have been growing this form from seed and have found it more tolerant to their conditions than any other form that they have tried. Perhaps this is the heat tolerant *R. occidentale* people have sought after. The Southern California Chapter of the ARS has also found this form of *R. occidentale* much more tolerant to dry air than any other form they have tried. It grows in canyons or boggy areas at elevations above 1370m that are heavily wooded with cedars. Their roots often run below boulders where precious moisture is preserved. The air is very dry and the relative humidity is often below 10%. Summer showers are few and far between; temperatures often go as high as 33°C. The flowers are almost pure white, about 6cm across and the characteristic yellow blotch is almost non-existent. The leaves are lanceolate and up to 11cm in length.

Bob Dunning moved to Maple Valley in 1978 and has been a volunteer and board member of Lake Wilderness Arboretum since 1997. When Britt and Jean Smith decided to sell their home in Kent, Washington and downsize, the Kent property was to be developed, meaning the loss of any plants left in the ground. A deal was struck with the developer allowing some of the Smiths's *R. occidentale* azalea collection to be relocated to Lake Wilderness Arboretum, formerly the South King County Arboretum near Maple Valley. Bob Dunning and his friend Dan Bailey worked tirelessly for four years to achieve the movement of the collection[3]. Frank Mossman also donated part of his collection to the arboretum. This part of the arboretum is now called the Smith-

DR FRANK MOSSMAN AT THE SMITH MOSSMAN GARDEN IN 2007
        BOB DUNNING*

R. 'MAGGIE BROWN' (a Frank Mossman hybrid) registered by Dick Cavender in 2008 and introduced by Briggs Nursery in 2009. It is named after a granddaughter of Frank Mossman
DICK CAVENDER

Mossman Western Azalea Garden which holds over 200 plants, the largest collection of *R. occidentale* selections in the world.

Dick (Red) Cavender is the owner of Red's Rhodies Nursery. On Red's first vacation with his wife Karen they went on a road trip to the Oregon Coast; during the trip, they drove by a flowering shrub growing by the side of the road. Red pulled over and got out to examine the flowers, they were white and fragrant with a clove like scent. This turned out to be *R. occidentale*, and so began the Cavenders' love of rhododendrons and azaleas. Red's Nursery business started as a hobby that got out of control. Red loves to hybridize to obtain new and improved varieties of *R. occidentale*, his favourite azalea. One of Red's ambitions is to produce large double flowers on *R. occidentale*. In 2006 he registered the double-flowered wild selection of Smith and Mossman, found on Crescent City Flats, California in 1966, as 'Crescent City Double'.

R. OCCIDENTALE SM030 'CRESCENT CITY GOLD'
JIM INSKIP

Mike Oliver is an engineer who became interested in rhododendrons, especially *R. occidentale*, when he moved to Oregon in 1980. In addition to searching for and collecting cuttings from unusual and attractive forms he has started intraspecific hybridizing. Mike's passion is to produce a pure yellow *R. occidentale* and often starts with SM30, which is still grown in the USA and has the most yellow on all five petals. For a number of years, he has contributed seed to the ARS seed exchange. Mike has been on many occidentale hunting trips in the wild along with Dick Cavender.

Mike McCulloch graduated from what was then San Jose State College (now San Jose State University) in 1970 with a BA in Social Science (a combination of history, political science, economics, sociology, and anthropology) and a

R. OCCIDENTALE SM028-2 'CRESCENT CITY DOUBLE'
KEN COX

R. OCCIDENTALE (P027 Patrick's Point 3806)

MIKE MCCULLOUGH

teaching minor in Philosophy. A few years after graduation he was in charge of the garden supply department of a Grants Department Store in San Jose. The description of rhododendrons in the Sunset Western Garden Book interested him. In May of 1975 he saw a mention in the San Jose Mercury about a rhododendron show being held in San Mateo by the San Mateo Chapter of the American Rhododendron Society, so he went and hasn't looked back since then!

For a period of over 30 years Mike McCulloch has explored a range extending from central Oregon to San Diego, California and has discovered many forms of R. occidentale. Mike continues to this day

R. OCCIDENTALE (Siskiyou 3901)   MIKE MCCULLOUGH

visiting every spring and again in the autumn to collect seeds that he has either pollinated or tagged. He tells me that sometimes it is the work of the two-legged pollinator that is most successful. Every year Mike sends details of his road trip with photos of himself and his companions and of course the R. occidentale they have seen.

A PISTILLATE FORM OF R. OCCIDENTALE   DICK CAVENDER

R. OCCIDENTALE MUTANTS

Over the years a number of R. occidentale mutant or pistillate forms have been found.

In 1974 H. J. Slonecker wrote an article in the ARS Bulletin on "Pistil Pete" and "Pistil Packin Mama" having been found at Myrtle Creek. Smith and Mossman discovered 'Miniskirt' 70 miles away at O'Brien, Oregon. The flowers are very small, only 9–12mm across[4].

R. OCCIDENTALE SM157 'MINISKIRT'   DICK CAVENDER

PROPAGATION

Seeds, cuttings, air or ground layers and grafting are all possible means of propagation. Seeds are the easiest but the slowest method of propagation;

R. 'WASHINGTON STATE CENTENNIAL'　　　　　　　　　　　　　　　　　HAROLD GREER

seeds can be obtained from the ARS seed list each year from wild collected sources, as the USA is not a signatory of the Nagoya Protocol. Cuttings can be difficult but it is the one way of accurately reproducing a particular plant. Layering is a slow process and is very successful, but lots of patience is required. Grafting is another good method but a plentiful supply of stocks is necessary.

R. 'EXQUISITUM'　　　　　　　　　DAVID MILLAIS

In the wild *R. occidentale* can tolerate a high pH in soils or water. In the Serpentine soils where *R. occidentale* grows, the pH of up to 8.5 is high, not because of calcium content but because of the magnesium and iron content. Experiments in the USA have used *R. occidentale* as grafting stocks onto which were successfully grafted Rhododendron scions[5].

R. OCCIDENTALE HYBRIDS

It was the importation of *R. occidentale* to the UK in 1850 that has ultimately given us the large flower size on our Knap Hill and Exbury hybrid deciduous azaleas. They are a useful addition to any garden as they are late flowering and scented. Many have wonderfully coloured leaves in the autumn. Equally, there are fine Dutch and Belgian hybrids too e.g. 'Irene Koster' and 'Exquisitum' from Koster's Nursery in Holland.

Hybridisation using *R. occidentale* in the USA has occurred much more recently; in fact it started nearly a hundred years after Waterer began his hybridising in the UK. A fine example of an American hybrid, registered by Frank Mossman, is *R.* 'Washington State Centennial'.

Another hybrid, perhaps more familiar to us in the UK is *R.* 'Jock Brydon'. This is a *molle* ssp. *molle* × *occidentale* hybrid developed by Dr Clausen and introduced by the Beneschoen Gardens at Myrtle Creek, Oregon.

R. 'JOCK BRYDON'   DAVID MILLAIS

WHERE TO SEE *R. OCCIDENTALE* IN THE USA

If you should be fortunate enough to be on the West coast of the USA at the right time of year, then here are a few of the places where you can see *R. occidentale*:

CALIFORNIA

Arcata-Azalea Reserve is a 30-acre tract near Arcata that was set aside as a State Park for the preservation of the Western Azalea.

Stagecoach Hill Azalea Reserve is a must, especially if you can only visit one place. The variations within this species can be seen at first hand.

R. OCCIDENTALE 'STAGECOACH PEPPERMINT'   JIM INSKIP

R. OCCIDENTALE 'STAGECOACH FRILLS'   BOB DUNNING*

OREGON

Brookings Azalea State Park is devoted almost exclusively to the care and preservation of *Rhododendron occidentale*. Brush and competing plants have been removed giving the azaleas a chance to develop at their best.

Harris Beach State Park is just north of Brookings. Many azaleas can be found in this area; unfortunately, widening and straightening the highway has resulted in the loss of many azaleas.

WASHINGTON

Lake Wilderness Arboretum is in Maple Valley, South East of Seattle. In addition to a focus on North West native plants, the Arboretum is home to the Smith Mossman Western Azalea Display Garden.

WHERE TO FIND *R. OCCIDENTALE* IN THE UK

Many of the hybrids of *R. occidentale* can be seen in public gardens in the UK and are readily available from garden centres and specialist nurseries for you to have and enjoy in your own gardens. The Dutch hybrid *R.* 'Irene Koster' is a great example of a readily available hybrid. The characteristics from its *R. occidentale* parentage are quite clear, as shown in the photo below *R. occidentale* is sold commercially in the UK but its availability is limited. *R. occidentale* SM028-2 'Crescent City Double' is also available in the UK.

To grow *R. occidentale* in UK gardens, humus rich, acid soil with a pH of 6.5 or less is needed and adequate, but not necessarily copious amounts of water for it to thrive. Humidity does appear to be an issue both in cultivation and in

R. 'IRENE KOSTER'

POLLY COOKE

R. OCCIDENTALE 'STAGECOACH CREAM'
(data.rbge.org.uk/living/19750138A)   RBG EDINBURGH

the wild; wild growing plants in coastal regions, with higher humidity, are taller than those growing inland where the humidity is lower[6]. R. occidentale will grow in full sun or partial shade but as it is a late flowering species, typically June, extreme heat will cause the flowers to collapse. Planting near water sources such as streams, ditches or ponds will improve the relative humidity near the flowers

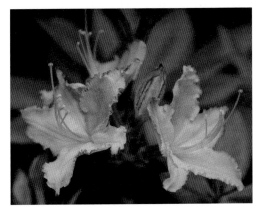

R. OCCIDENTALE grown from wild-collected material
(data.rbge.org.uk/living/19741728A)   RBG EDINBURGH

and extend the flowering period significantly. Normally in cultivation in the UK it will grow to approximately 1.5m in 10 years but its growth will be much more vigorous if planted in damp areas. R. occidentale does need an open well

ventilated aspect to prevent the occurrence of powdery mildew from late summer onwards. In the wild R. occidentale can survive through winters in southern Oregon and northern California while it is covered in snow for several months, so it is a hardy plant and our UK winters should not have a detrimental effect on this species. It is unlikely that R. occidentale will tolerate alkaline soil in this country, as the alkalinity is due to the calcium content, whereas in the US the alkalinity is due to the magnesium and iron content of the mafic soils.

It is the view of Mike Oliver that R. occidentale also needs the correct mycorrhiza to prosper: "Ericaceous plants need the association of the mycorrhiza hymenoscyphus ericae to prosper at all. If the strains of this in the west coast of the USA and in Europe are compatible with R. occidentale they will grow, but if the strains available are not compatible, they will not grow. It should be noted that another ericaceous plant, R. macrophyllum, grows in the west but is unable to grow in the south-eastern US".[6] Clearly further investigation is needed here in order to confirm if the geographical limitations we see are caused by mycorrhizal association or by some other mechanism.

Regrettably there aren't many collections of R. occidentale in the UK but you may find a few plants in some public gardens in England. There are two collections that I know of in Scotland. Glendoick Gardens have a collection and you will notice that Ken Cox has contributed some great photos for this article. The Royal Botanic Garden Edinburgh also holds a good sized collection.

In his book published in 1995, H. H. Davidian records that "in 1975 Mr A. Tatum sent six named clones of *R. occidentale* to RBG Edinburgh"[7], including 'Stagecoach Cream'. You can see from the data accession details given under the photo, that this plant was introduced in 1975. The photo was taken in 2013.

As you have seen there are incredible variations in the flowers of *Rhododendron occidentale* growing in the wild. These are all natural, as there are no other deciduous azaleas at all growing in the region. It is entirely due to the eye for detail of all of the plant hunters mentioned above that we have such a varied selection of this species to admire. You will have noticed that the flowers in some photographs are white with a yellow blotch which is typical of *R. occidentale*. It is the small differences in each of these that the plant hunters have noticed, recorded and collected seed from for propagation and further study.

There is one more variant that I must share with you. I have only seen it in this photo from Ken Cox, SM303 – gorgeous isn't it!

R. OCCIDENTALE SM303   **KEN COX**

If you are interested in seeing more photos of *R. occidentale*, then you should go online to www.smith-mossman.net

You will find an extraordinary photographic resource compiled by Bob Dunning.

The photos credited to Bob Dunning marked * have been reproduced, with consent, from Bob's website: www.smith-mossman.net

Two of these, *R. occidentale* SM042 and 'Stagecoach Frills' are Bob's scans of Britt Smiths original slides taken before the birth of digital photography. These photos have been digitally enhanced by Barry Cooke.

RBGE kindly gave permission for the reproduction of their photos providing that the accession data was included.

With many thanks to Dick (Red) Cavender, Polly and Barry Cooke, Ken Cox, Bob Dunning, Harold Greer, Mike McCulloch, David Millais, Molly Nilsson, Mike Oliver, Pacific Horticulture, Sally Perkins, Royal Botanic Gardens Edinburgh and Tim Walsh.

REFERENCES:

1. Exploring the Ploidy by John and Sally Perkins, The Azalean 37/12
2. *Rhododendron occidentale* Survey by Leonard F. Frisbie, Rhododendron April 1967
3. Dedication of the Smith-Mossman Western Azalea Garden by Bob Dunning JARS v54n4
4. Smith-Mossman Western Azalea Garden by Rick Peterson and Richie Steffen, Pacific Horticulture April 2010
5. The Slosson Reports:
slosson.ucdavis.edu/newsletters/Reid_199829064.pdf
slosson.ucdavis.edu/newsletters/Reid_199929051.pdf
6. Personal Communication from Mike Oliver
7. The Rhododendron Species Volume IV Azaleas by H.H. Davidian (1995)

JIM INSKIP

is a member of the Wessex Branch Committee of the RCMG. He is interested in all deciduous azaleas but his main focus is with Ghent Azaleas. His hobby is the propagation and study of deciduous azaleas

Mahee Island – from a Barren Drumlin to a Woodland Garden

The year in Mahee's 2018 calendar has seen many things, but none as rewarding as the visit in April by the Rhododendron, Camellia & Magnolia group of the RHS.

Their visit followed a relentless stormy winter and a late spring, but mercifully they came before the equally relentless five weeks of drought. These climatic events caused alarm and some despondency, but on the whole and with characteristic resilience, the rhododendrons and camellias are looking themselves again although for some of the younger magnolias, only time will tell.

It was during this delightful and instructive visit that I was made aware of the importance of documenting the transformation of what in 1959 had been a portion of a barren island into the woodland garden it has become.

This then is how it began.

In 1959, aged 28 and recently married to Julie, I had the great good fortune to be given a site by my father-in-law Lance Turtle to build a house. It was situated on the top of a bare hill at the end of Mahee Island, Strangford Lough, located 20 miles southeast of Belfast. Lance had been coming to Mahee since the 1920s when it really was the back of beyond. There was a causeway to the island, but no electricity and only a spring-fed well for water. The rocky road along the shore to his holiday cottage was at the mercy of the tides that had to be carefully negotiated twice a day.

In 1959, although the road from Belfast had improved, there were still no utility services to make the building of a house an idyllic prospect. However, in the spring of 1960, electricity did

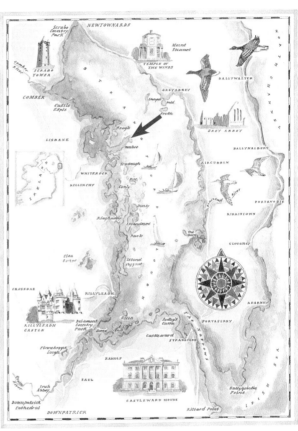

STRANGFORD LOUGH SHOWING MAHEE ISLAND   JOANNA MARTIN

arrive, an artesian well was being bored and the foundations of the house were being laid. There was also a plan to raise the rocky road, thus avoiding the inconvenience and drama of being tide-bound.

Luckily, in anticipation of all this happening, I had applied for a Planting Grant from the Ministry of Agriculture, Northern Ireland. My objective was to build up enough shelter on this exposed island so that I could eventually plant the collection of *Rhododendron* seedlings that I

MAHEE ISLAND IN 1960 WITH SHELTER BELTS UNDERWAY

PADDY MACKIE

My planting years had begun and in February 1960, 200 *Betula pendula* (silver birch) and 100 *Salix alba* var. *vitellina* 'Britzensis' (scarlet willow) were delivered as well as 400 *Larix kaempferi* (Japanese larch) under the auspices of the Young Tree Scheme. The 'over four acres' were soon to become thirty-five. At this time, I met the department's Head Forester Alfie Rogers, who came to inspect the planting. He reported that the young trees had been well planted and despite the exposure, only five had succumbed. This was the beginning of a long friendship and collaboration, without which Mahee might not have the diversity of planting that we achieved.

had in a cold frame at my previous home. I duly filled out the Government's Prospective Form for 'over four acres', and when this was accepted, the following trees, chosen for the benefit of their resistance to wind-borne salt damage, were supplied at a cost of £41.13.0.

   1,900 *Pinus sylvestris* (Scots pine)
   3,500 *Pinus nigra* (Corsican pine)
   1,700 *Acer pseudoplatanus* (sycamore)

The exposure of the island was always the main consideration when planning the planting programme. Later in 1960, Daisy Hill Nurseries in County Down supplied *Pinus radiata* (Monterey pine), and my first order to Benjamin Reid in Aberdeen was for *Acer platanoides* (Norway maple), *Prunus avium* (common cherry), *Aesculus hippocastanum* (horse chestnut) and *Malus domestica* (apple trees). I was always sure that Benjamin Reid would become my main supplier in that their

MAHEE ISLAND FROM THE AIR, 2008

BRYAN RUTLEDGE

conditions, being even more challenging than mine, might ensure the success of the project. I suggested that perhaps *Pinus sylvestris* 'Loch Maree' (Scots pine) would do well here and was delighted when the Nursery collected seed that they then propagated for me. I was grateful when, in the event of being unable to supply me with a given species, they kindly referred me to Messrs. T&W Christie Nurserymen, Forres, or Christie (Fochabers) Ltd, also in Scotland, or R. Williams Ellis of Glasfryn Forest Nursery in Wales. These recommendations were followed up most satisfactorily and the resulting *Cupressus macrocarpa* (Monterey cypress) to this day provide a sheltered winter roost for the Little Egrets that arrived a few years ago from further south. It is interesting to be reminded of the varied transportation arrangements of the 1960s. In December 1960, in a letter to Christies (Fochabers), I stipulated that there shouldn't be any straw in the packing as there were restrictions on trees coming into Northern Ireland and the Veterinary Department insisted that trees should be handled as vegetables! Burns Laird was the shipping line chosen at that time by Scottish Nurseries. Northern Ireland also had many good sources for the trees that I needed. Tollymore and Castlewellan Forest Parks were constantly helpful as were the Slieve Donard and Daisy Hill nurseries.

Early on, I was aware that *Eucalyptus* would be significant additions to my overall planting scheme and I was fortunate to be given seeds by an Australian friend who acquired them from the Australian Commonwealth Scientific Institute Research Organisation. Seeds from nine species duly arrived, which I propagated successfully in the greenhouse. Alfie Rogers also drew my attention to his surplus at Tollymore that I planted on the North Bank. We agreed that they were not only beautiful but fast growing. They have also proved their worth given their ability to bend rather than break in high winds, and to filter rather than attempt to block the gales. *Pinus radiata* (Monterey pine) also had these important characteristics, unlike maritime pines that were badly affected by the severe easterly gales. Another species planted in the early years, at my insistence, was beech, but this was contrary to expert advice at the time which has since proved to be unfounded.

My aunt, Vera Mackie of Guincho, County Down, who discovered *Sambucus nigra* f. *porphyrophylla* 'Guincho Purple' (elder 'Guincho Purple'), was an extremely important and early mentor. She was so delighted to have a nephew who shared my passion for plants that she was unstinting in her encouragement and advice: she gave me my first *Kniphofia uvaria* 'Nobilis' (redhot poker 'Nobilis') knowing of their stiff, self-supporting stems and their wind and salt tolerance; a book she recommended was 'Seaside Gardening' by Christine Kelway, which became a well-thumbed favourite; when my *Eucalyptus gunnii* (cider gum) were beginning to stretch, she suggested that they should be docked so that their branches would fork and their roots go deeper – this advice has proved to be invaluable as few have been lost. (On the other hand, *Eucalyptus viminalis*, the drooping gum variety, wasn't as fortunate.) As she was one of the key Northern Ireland members of the Inter-

RHODODENDRON 'HORIZON MONARCH'   PADDY MACKIE

national Dendrology Society, I now realise that the plantsman she brought to Mahee in 1962 would probably have been its President. Being such a novice in the early 1960s, I wouldn't have had sufficient knowledge of this august organisation to realise the importance of the visit. I certainly do now.

My archives indicate that 1962/3 were the years of the most intensive planting. I wrote to the many nurseries who advertised in the RHS magazine asking for their catalogues to be sent. (I sometimes sent 3d to cover postage.) Very few of those I contacted are in business today, although it's interesting to learn that Reuthes Nursery in Sevenoaks, founded in 1902 by an Austrian plant hunter, is thriving (www.reuthes.com).

PADDY MACKIE AND PETER COX ADMIRE THE *RHODODENDRON SINOGRANDE*

JULIE MACKIE

I also came across a letter in the magazine requesting recruitment assistance. Its member-ship in 1964 was 66,000 but *an increase would be beneficial for the cost of printing the Journal as well as the upkeep of Wisley.* In the same year, I wrote to Mr P. M. Synge requesting back numbers of the Rhododendron Year Books from 1946 to 1962; obviously a sign of things to come.

The shelter belts had fulfilled their purpose and Mahee had been transformed. There were, of course, the inevitable losses mainly because of their vulnerability to the strong prevailing winds. Hares were culprits, too, as they nibbled most, if not all, the leaders of the 1,700 *Acer pseudoplatanus* (sycamore) that had been planted in 1960. The hard winter of 1962/3 also caused casualties, and instead of the tides, the snow-bound rocky road reminded me that we could still be in the back of beyond.

My earlier quest for trees had been succeeded by a different form of plant hunting and, once again, Scotland became my inspiration. The Cox family of Glendoick, Perthshire, with their unsurpassed knowledge of all things rhodo-dendron, has been central to this transformation. Euan Cox was not only a plant hunter and author but he also came from a jute background, similar to mine. In fact, my family supplied his with

textile machinery, as his now supplied me with rhododendrons. In 1951, I remember being at a textile exhibition in the Caird Hall, Dundee, where I met Hope Pilcher, the Chairman of Jute Industries. I can only imagine that we must have had a conversation about plants as well as about the Pony Spinning Frame that I was exhibiting, because he took me to Glendoick where Euan met us. I remember also that there were beds of camellias round the front door. In 1953, Glendoick Garden opened, and a rhododendron nursery followed a year later. Two further generations of intrepid plant hunters have made sure that the Cox name is still paramount.

When Peter Cox and his son Ken visited Mahee in 2017, Peter remarked when a photograph was taken with us beside *Rhododendron sinogrande* (great Chinese rhododendron), that he had, in all probability, collected its seed in China. He also remarked that he had never seen one that was flowering so prolifically. I suggested that this might be down to the low rainfall at Mahee, which put certain plants under stress and therefore into a flowering survival regime. Peter had gone a long way to collect this seed and Mahee had come a long way too.

As well as the shelter belts of the early 1960s, my interest in waterfowl and their conservation on Strangford Lough continued. When building the house on the then treeless Mahee, the spoil from its foundations was used to create a barrage at the point of the island and so blocked off a

WINTER 2010 – *DICKSONIA ANTARCTICA*   PADDY MACKIE

Himalaya. Lady Leitrim's Mulroy Estate, another influence, also benefited from these early introductions to Ireland which include *R. arboreum* (tree-like rhododendron), *R. barbatum* (bearded rhododendron), *R. falconeri* (Falconer rhododendron), *R. niveum* (snowy rhododendron) and *R. sinogrande* (grand Chinese rhododendron). All are thriving on Mahee today, an undoubted outcome of my visits to these two important places.

Near Ardnamona is the even more famous Glenveagh Estate, where Henry McIlhenny began to develop the gardens in the late 1940s. He was assisted by Jim Russell of Sunningdale Nurseries and Lanning Roper, his Harvard classmate, both well-known garden design consultants. My father got to know Henry McIlhenny through a mutual friend, the artist Frank Egginton, who fished in Lough Veagh with Henry. I didn't fish, but I did have an introduction to his magnificent garden and determined that I,

small tidal inlet. This became an effective freshwater pond, so effective in fact that when I constructed catching cages with a view to having a waterfowl ringing station, little did I know then how many thousands of duck and waders (29,000) would be caught and ringed over the next 40 years with the official rings of the British Trust for Ornithology. This was a contribution to the then unknown destinations of their migratory range. Ringing returns have resulted in increasing our knowledge considerably: wigeon and pintail come from Russia; teal from the Baltic; and redshank from Iceland.

In 1969, another pond was created – this time, on the front lawn of the house. It has become a favourite watering hole for the feral flock of Strangford Lough's barnacle geese. Up to 400 can fly in at any given time of the day and night, and what a pleasure it is to see them on their flight path as they navigate over the trees that once were a mere 9in high, but now form a significant foreground to the lough.

I now realise that my interests have come full circle and my planting continues wholly due to the influences that I have experienced over many years. One of the first was Ardnamona Estate in County Donegal, Ireland, where George and Charlotte Wray planted a pinetum in the 1850s. Rhododendrons followed and when I visited in the late 1950s, there were hundreds of species, subspecies and hybrids, many planted shortly after they were introduced from China and the

BARNACLE GEESE ON THE FRONT LAWN   JULIE MACKIE

too, must have a *Cercidiphyllum japonicum* (katsura tree).

Another friend of my father's was Ambrose Congreve, whose large-scale woodland garden in County Waterford, Ireland, was a source of wonder with its magnificent swathe of magnolias being a showstopper. He tells of Ambrose inspecting his creation on horseback. In his latter years, the horse gave way to a golf buggy, but Ambrose's enthusiasm never dimmed and he lived to 104, dying on his way to the Chelsea Flower Show where he had won 13 Gold Medal Awards for Mount Congreve. As Ambrose was influenced by Exbury, in Hampshire, the famous Rothschild Gardens, so was I by Ambrose as I now have a very substantial *Magnolia* collection. Leonardslee Gardens in West Sussex, England, and Mount Usher in County Wicklow, Ireland, are two other wonderful examples of superb planting, both of which have influenced me over the years.

RHODODENDRON EDGEWORTHII

PADDY MACKIE

I have already mentioned the Cox family, who continue to inspire and inform me with their visits, and to whose many distinguished books I constantly refer. The Late Patrick Forde, a remarkable plant hunter and plantsman of local fame, whose Seaforde Estate in County Down holds the National Collection of *Euchryphia*, also supplied me with many of the rhododendrons he collected. A more recent supplier is John Gault from County Londonderry who at the age of 3 caught the rhododendron bug from which he has never recovered.

As with all great gardens, every visit generates ideas of what to do and sometimes what not to do. I am mindful of the dangers of over planting or of omitting to bite the bullet of the occasional and necessary cull. Every year, I try to be dispassionate about difficult decisions as I raise crowns, lop off branches or frequently take down a healthy specimen that unfortunately is blocking the light that impacts on the shrub below. Not making these essential decisions has sometimes been detrimental to both tree and shrub. I am convinced that giving them their

own space has been one of the most important lessons I have learned. Inevitably, as trees blossomed and flourished, views would gradually disappear. At first, I found it extremely hard to dispatch handsome specimens that had served me so well but to lose a tantalising glimpse of the Lough would have been even harder, so after the first chop, and the results noticed, my task became easier as new and exciting vistas opened up. Occasionally, however, nature takes decisions for me. Although *Eucalyptus johnstonii* (Tasmanian yellow gum), with its distinctive barley sugar bark, survived the winters of 2010/11, sadly, *Pinus montezumae* var. *montezumae*, which survived those two winters of prolonged frosts, succumbed to easterly gales with torrential rains in January 2013. During those disastrous winters, temperatures were below Mahee's lowest of -7 degrees Celsius. However, in a particularly sheltered spot there were groupings of stoic *Dicksonia antarctica* (Australian tree fern) and New Zealand's *Dicksonia fibrosa* (golden or woolly tree fern) – all of which survived these unusual extremes.

Yet another important lesson I have learned is to mulch frequently. I think that many plants have been able to defy this year's prolonged drought because of the moisture retention properties of the bark mulch I have lavished on them. And there is always the importance of labelling, which I learnt from my father, preferring, as he did, the method of

ACER PALMATUM 'BLOODGOOD' AND *LIRIODENDRON TULIPIFERA*   PADDY MACKIE

punching out a plant's particulars – species, provenance and date of planting – onto an aluminium strip.

In 1990, the remarkable Thomas Pakenham founded The Irish Tree Society to increase public and private appreciation of specimen trees in Ireland, and I became a member in 1991. Its annual programme consists of visits to gardens and estates all over Ireland as well as a foray every spring to pastures new in Britain and Europe. I have benefited more than I can say from these trips. Knowledge and enthusiasm is always generously shared by our hosts, and Mahee, I hope, has become a glimmer of many exceptional gardens, both large and small being equally beautiful. Although Mahee's shelter-belt planting wasn't planned as an arboretum, it has perhaps with the acquisition of more interesting and specialised trees become to resemble one, and with the success of the *Rhododendron*, *Camellia* and *Magnolia* underplanting, and much else besides, even a woodland garden has emerged.

I am honoured that our esteemed family friend Seamus O'Brien of the National Botanic Gardens, Kilmacurragh, County Wicklow, has allowed me to use his succinct overview of Mahee's arboreal beginning. Seamus has seen most of my rhododendrons in the wild and has published distinguished books on two of the great plant hunters; Augustine Henry and Joseph Hooker. In 2018, he was awarded the Royal Horticultural Society of Ireland's Gold Medal of Honour.

'*The Woodland garden at Mahee is of some 35 acres on a drowned drumlin on the west side of Strangford Lough, near Killyleagh where Sir Hans Sloane spent his childhood. Another point of historical interest is Nendrum Abbey on Mahee which has the remains of the earliest known dated Tidal Corn Mill in the world dating back to 619 AD.*

The point of the island points directly across the Lough to Mount Stewart which shares Mahee's micro climate allowing tender shrubs to thrive.

Half a century ago Paddy Mackie moved to the island, then with a single ash tree. His immediate priority was to establish shelter which today

MEMORIAL CAIRN ON THE POINT OF MAHEE ISLAND

PADDY MACKIE

protects the garden from winter storms and strong coastal winds.

Visitors to Mahee little realise that this is the lifework of a single individual. This corner of County Down has a benign climate, one of the mildest on the island of Ireland, and many of the exotic trees planted by Paddy, particularly the Eucalyptus and Eucryphia species look far older than they really are. The mild climate permits the cultivation of a wide range of tender subjects and southern hemisphere plants like echiums, tree ferns and proteas, though it is for its Rhododendron collection that Mahee is best known. Probably the best privately owned collection in Northern Ireland, the collection is centered on choice species and tender hybrids. Many of the species are of wild origin and the collection is fully documented.

Rhododendron sinogrande has reached dimensions similar to those found in western China and there are also fine free-flowering specimens of newly introduced species like R. heatheriae from southeast Tibet and R. kesangiae, named for the Queen Grandmother of Bhutan. Camellias from the Slieve Donard Nursery planted from 1964, complement the rhododendrons as do 60 species of magnolia planted from 1998.'

Although I have never been a plant hunter in the accepted sense of that description, I suspect that my daughter, Tara, is right when she said that I am "a plant hunter in my own back garden". She also said to include my cousin, Gordon Mackie's, poem about Mahee, to remind me how determined I once was and still am.

To describe the trees of Mahee
as a wood, takes no account
of the tireless determination
that creates a forest garden,
on a bare scald of a drumlin.

PADDY MACKIE
worked as a textile engineer in Belfast and founded Castle Espie Conservation Centre in 1982 – now Wildfowl & Wetlands Trust, Castle Espie

A New Zealand overview

RHODODENDRON DELL AT DUNEDIN BOTANIC GARDEN

WILLIAM STANGER

Following horticultural training, including an MA in Historic Designed Landscapes, and three years with The Professional Gardeners' Guild Traineeship, incorporating placements at Thenford Arboretum, Savill Garden and The Garden House, I started to plan a trip to New Zealand and apply for funding. From September 2017, I spent a year travelling around New Zealand and worked in various gardens such as Dunedin Botanic Garden, Pukeiti and Ayrlies. Placements ranged from a week to three months. Some of the key aims of my trip were to study the native flora, and to visit New Zealand gardens and horticulturists. I wanted to learn more about big leaf rhododendrons, and hybrids of rhododendrons and magnolias bred in New Zealand. As well as working with notable rhododendron collections like the Rhododendron

Dell at Dunedin Botanic Garden and Pukeiti, I visited specialist nurseries such as Woodbury Rhododendron Nursery owned by Bernie and Joy O'Keefe, and Blue Mountain Nursery owned by Denis Hughes. Bernie, Joy and Denis are key plantspeople who play an instrumental role in the conservation work of New Zealand hybrid rhododendrons and have bred notable selections themselves. The New Zealand Rhododendron Association Conference is a major highlight in the rhododendron year for New Zealand and for me it presented an opportunity to see more gardens including Cross Hills and Heritage Park. At the same time, I was able to meet rhododendron enthusiasts who suggested other gardens and people to visit. A full report of the trip can be obtained from the RHS Wisley Library and the Merlin Trust.

Working in New Zealand gardens has given me an insight into some of the challenges the country's horticulturists face. Because of the stronger light intensity, exotic plants in New Zealand photosynthesise more, and thus grow more quickly. At first this may seem to be an advantage, but it also means that plants reach maturity and complete their senescence more quickly. For some exotic plants the climate in New Zealand is more favourable and they become weeds, such as *Tropaeolum speciosum*. Then there is the ongoing battle with destructive possums. Another consideration is that although New Zealand gardeners can grow more tender species than those in the UK, it is also more challenging to grow species that require a dormant period or a defined cold winter. After working with New Zealand rhododendron collections and speaking with the people who cultivate them, I have acquired a greater knowledge of the history of growing rhododendrons in New Zealand, and which hybrids are most garden worthy. This article is a summary of my findings.

Rhododendrons are a prime example of how plants can play a role in international relationships. It is well known that gardeners are keen to pass on their knowledge and share plants, and this is highly evident in how the first rhododendrons were brought to New Zealand. The resultant hybrids were shared and improved by each subsequent generation. Today, New Zealand has a rich history of rhododendron hybrids, and steps are now being taken to conserve them for future generations to enjoy.

The rhododendron story of New Zealand begins with William Martin, who came to New Zealand in the passenger ship *Philip Laing* in April 1848. Martin was trained as a nurseryman at the Royal Botanic Garden Edinburgh and wasted no time in starting a nursery in his new homeland. He is credited with introducing the first rhododendrons to the Otago region. Unfortunately, there appears to be no record of what species were imported or where they came from. Of the hybrids raised by William Martin, *Rhododendron* 'Marquis of Lothian' (*thomsonii* × *griffithianum*) is considered the very best. The reverse cross 'Cornish Cross' (*griffithianum* × *thomsonii*) is similar, but 'Marquis of Lothian' is held to be superior, or at least in New Zealand. It

has wonderful cinnamon-coloured peeling bark, the flowers are held in a lax truss and are reddish pink on the outside with a pronounced darker flushed edge, and paler pink within. It prefers a sheltered position away from draughts and needs protection from direct sunlight. I saw a marvellous specimen at Dunedin Botanic Garden in full bloom.

Edgar Stead was the owner of Ilam Homestead in Christchurch and was a keen rhododendron enthusiast. Writing in 1947, he noted how few rhododendrons were in New Zealand prior to 1915. There were some Himalayan species including *Rhododendron griffithianum, R. arboreum, R. grande, R. barbatum, R. falconeri* and *R. thomsonii*. In about 1860, Sir Cracroft Wilson, a magistrate from Manipur in India, settled near Christchurch, bringing with him seed of a red form of *R. arboreum*. Two of the resultant seedlings had large trusses of deep blood red flowers, and eventually the best specimen was moved to Edgar's home at Ilam, dodging overhead tramlines. Later still, this *arboreum* was was reclassified as a hybrid now known as *R.* 'Noyo Chief'. A spark of interest in rhododendrons in New Zealand was created by the publication of *Rhododendrons and the Various Hybrids* by J. G. Millais. This led to more frequent importations into New Zealand, including seed of Chinese species, and in 1925 Edgar travelled to England. Here he obtained a collection of rhododendrons from various sources including Lionel de Rothschild and Lady Loder. Following this, many more plants were imported and introduced to commerce.

Edgar began hybridising in 1918 and in his 1947 article he goes into some detail of the crosses he made and the results. One of his more notable, between *Rhododendron fortunei* ssp. *fortunei* and *R. griffithianum,* repeated the famous Loderi Group cross and resulted in 'Irene Stead' and 'Ilam Cream'. Both have the classic characteristics of a Loderi rhododendron. 'Irene Stead' has a large truss of 12–14 soft lilac-pink flowers with darker colouring on the edges; the colour does not fade. 'Ilam Cream' grows into a large tree-like shrub that prefers some overhead shade; the huge deep cream corollas have a delicate band of rose pink around their edges. The sweet scent and sheer size of the flower makes it a firm favourite.

In the same article, Stead also describes his work with azaleas. In 1917 he received seeds of various North American deciduous azaleas from Professor C. S. Sargent, including three selections of *Rhododendron calendulaceum*. In 1925 he obtained plants from Anthony Waterer's breeding programme from Knap Hill Nurseries. During a visit to Exbury in 1930, Lionel de Rothschild allowed Edgar to make crosses among the azaleas, and the seed was sent back to him in New Zealand. The resultant seedlings were then themselves crossed with Waterer's plants and also with Mollis azaleas as an outcross. This produced plants with new colours, increased truss size and fragrance, although only the lighter coloured hybrids were fragrant. It is also said that the flowers have substance and are usually more durable in hot weather (Millar, 2015). It is still possible to visit Ilam Homestead, which is now part of the University of Canterbury, and see the plants that Edgar bred and used in his breeding programme. I visited at the beginning of October when many of the Ilam hybrid azaleas were in full bloom, along with other rhododendron hybrids bred by Edgar Stead. Kathryn Millar clarified that the plants were never named in Stead's day, and the original plantings have now been supplemented with modern commercial hybrids.

Dr John Yeates continued Edgar's breeding work on the Ilam azaleas. With what he learnt from Edgar, he was able to select plants with yellow or orange flowers in full trusses and with frilled petals. Many of them have been registered and are known as the Melford hybrids. Dr Salinger (1994) describes Dr Yeates's time at Massey Agricultural College and his involvement with the beginnings of the NZRA (New Zealand Rhododendron Association) in 1944. Dr Yeates was the initial Secretary-Treasurer of the Association, a position he held for 21 years. He was also largely responsible for convincing Edgar to be its first President.

Dr Yeates also initiated the idea of a demonstration ground. Consequently, what is now known as Heritage Park at Kimbolton was bought by the Association in 1970. Plants and propagation material were imported from Exbury, Royal Botanical Garden Edinburgh, RHS Wisley, Bodnant and commercial nurserymen in the UK and the USA. At the Hocken Library in Dunedin, I was fortunate to see original letters to Dr Yeates from Leonard F. Frisbie (American Rhododendron Society) dated around 1948, that discuss the merits of Edgar's azaleas, and which rhododendrons to send over from the USA. There is also a letter from Sir Eric Savill thanking Dr Yeates for lily bulbs and azaleas. The majority of letters that I saw, show the correspondence between Dr Yeates and Frank Kingdon-Ward in relation to sponsoring plant hunting trips and the seed being sent to New Zealand. It is possible to get a sense of the difficulties of getting permission to undertake plant hunting trips at the time and also the perils of plant hunting in general. The letters range from 1948–68. [The NZRA Bulletins 2003 and 2005 contain more information on the Frank Kingdon-Ward letters and plant hunting in general (Millar and Morten, 2003 and 2005).]

LETTER TO DR YEATES FROM FRANK KINGDON-WARD, 1952
HOCKEN LIBRARY, DUNEDIN

CROWN ESTATE OFFICE
THE GREAT PARK, WINDSOR, BERKS
Telephone and Telegrams: Windsor 602/3

16th July, 1960

Dear Dr. Yeates,

Thank you so very much for your letter of 1st instant.
I am only just able to deal with it, for I have been away on
leave and returned only yesterday.

The rooted cuttings of Azaleas arrived in perfect
condition, and they have been individually potted up so as to
encourage a certain amount of growth before our winter commences,
and I shall keep them indoors, under cold conditions, until our
next spring.

I am so grateful to you for this generous present, half of
which is, of course, for Lady Freyberg.

I note with great pleasure that you propose to send a few
of your Lily bulbs, later on.

With very best wishes,
Yours sincerely,

Eric Savill

Dr. J. S. Yeates,
The New Zealand Rhododendron Association,
Massey College,
Palmerston North,
New Zealand.

by air mail

LETTER FROM ERIC SAVILL TO DR YEATES, 1960 **HOCKEN LIBRARY, DUNEDIN**

Mollie Coker and her first husband Ivan D. Wood, became a neighbour of Edgar Stead in the Christchurch suburb of Ilam. She was another Rhododendron enthusiast, and was highly influenced by Edgar, and used many of his hybrids, especially Loderi cultivars, in her own breeding programme. (Coker, 2017). Her first registered hybrid was of this stable and was registered by the NZRA as *Rhododendron* 'Mollie Coker'. This tree-like plant with large dark leaves, has bright pink fragrant flowers in a large compact truss. The corollas are large and frilled, with a wine-red throat. Among the thirteen hybrids that Mollie registered are additional Loderi-type hybrids such as 'The Dream' and 'Phantom'. The seed she obtained from the USA resulted in named hybrids such as 'Ivan D. Wood', named after her first husband, 'Coral Queen' and 'Pacific Princess'. *Rhododendron* 'Ivan D. Wood' is an upright open bush, strong growing and

prefers a little shade. The flowers have a cream-green edge with an orange-buff centre fading to Naples yellow, and are carried in a well-proportioned truss. *R.* 'Coral Queen' also likes some shade; it has an open habit growing to about 1.5m in 10 years, and its large reddish buds open to deep coral, openly campanulate flowers in a loose truss.

Brian Coker, Mollie's nephew, told me about Mollie's rhododendrons and his role as New Zealand Rhododendron Registrar. One of his challenges is to encourage people to register their hybrids, but filling in the paperwork and gathering all the details at flowering time coincides with a busy time of year. Unfortunately, Brian lost both his legs in the 2011 Christchurch earthquake, but this has not stopped him and his wife Helen creating a new garden at West Melton, south of Christchurch. As well as rhododendrons, camellias and magnolias, Brian and Helen have a diverse garden including herbaceous perennials and woody planting. The overall feel is of an English Country Garden. The garden has been designed with flat paths and low walls on which Brian can sit. They were able to move a number of plants from their previous garden. The garden at the time of writing is just four and a half years' old and has yet to develop adequate tree cover for shade loving plants. The lack of rainfall in the Christchurch area is also problematic, particularly for larger leaved rhododendrons. They record all their plants on a spreadsheet, and iCloud has made this easier. When I visited, they had recorded 200 rhododendrons and 800 other plants.

Mollie was very generous in how she shared her plant material. Consequently, many more of her hybrids were grown on and registered by others. Graham and Helen Holmes registered a number of them; *Rhododendron* 'Lalique', a Loderi type, being considered one of the best. It is a vigorous round plant that prefers shade and grows to 2m in 10 years with long shiny leaves, but it is inclined to sprawl rather than be upright. The beautiful flowers start neon-rose and fade to white, and are sweetly scented in large trusses. Mollie also worked on the Ilam azaleas which in turn were further developed by Denis Hughes who named a red one 'Mollie'.

Denis Hughes studied Horticulture at Lincoln University, near Christchurch, where a friend there had a traditional quarter-acre section with a glasshouse. Not far away was Mollie Coker's garden, where Denis and his friend worked at weekends and learnt about azaleas from her. After leaving college, Denis obtained azalea cuttings from Mollie and was thus able to get the best Ilam azalea varieties. His in-laws went to Chelsea Flower Show where they saw the impressive stand put on by Waterer's nursery and purchased Ghent and double Knap Hill azaleas. However, the transition from Northern to Southern Hemisphere gave the double azaleas jet lag. Their first flowers were single which meant Denis could use them more easily for hybridising with Ilam azaleas. Once the Knap Hill azaleas had recovered they flowered normally with double flowers.

Rhododendron 'Pavlova' came from that first cross and is a strong growing upright azalea with clean green, mildew-resistant foliage, good autumn colour, and double white scented flowers. The second generation (F2) resulted in a double flower that was still able to set seed and looked like a tutu of a ballet girl. 'Ballet Girl' is not registered but is a parent of many progeny such as 'Nicholas de Rothschild'. 'Nicholas de Rothschild' has small but distinctive scented flowers which are red in bud, opening golden yellow and changing to pink. My personal favourite is 'Soft Lights' whose flowers are held in a full ball-shaped truss, and are a combination of cream, peach, and apricot blended with pink. The flowers are paler when grown in shade, and vibrant pink in the sun.

Denis continued to work with Stead's red azaleas but came up with nothing better. Later, by chance he got a red azalea from Exbury, and he crossed this with the best Ilam red azaleas to produce an F1 strain with bigger red flowers. For some reason it is proving very difficult to produce a red double azalea. Denis has been running Blue Mountain Nursery in Otago, for nearly 60 years

RHODODENDRON 'LALIQUE'   **WILLIAM STANGER**

but in that time, azaleas have not been the only plant he has worked with. He has amassed an impressive collection of *Sophora* native to New Zealand, one of the most notable being *S. molloyi* 'Dragon's Gold'. One cannot make a quick visit to see Denis, he has a lot of knowledge to pass on and does so with a great deal of enthusiasm. We spent a good few hours looking around the nursery and discussing his work.

Another nurseryman, Jeff Elliott, was also influenced by Mollie and Edgar. His mentor was the Australian Professor E. G. Waterhouse who established his Camellia Grove Nursery in a Sydney suburb in 1939. Jeff started Elliotts Wholesale Nursery in 1980, north of Christchurch, and has been hybridising rhododendrons since his early 20s. Olives and feijoas are some of his staples, but Jeff has always had a passion for rhododendrons, and he continues to propagate and sell thousands each year. *Rhododendron* 'Kiwi Magic' was one of his first hybrids that began the Kiwi series. Apart from being prone to fertiliser damage and a poor root system, 'Kiwi Magic' has proved to be a good plant. It is best described as an orangey *R. yakushimanum* hybrid. *R.* 'Kiwi Pearl' has full round trusses of rich cream flowers accompanied by thick dark green leaves. Although sometimes difficult to establish, it has proven to be a good plant for the hot east coast regions of New Zealand. *R.* 'Kiwi Mum' has creamy peach flowers growing up to 1.2m, but Jeff admitted its foliage and root system are not the best.

Jeff told me the aims of his breeding programme and what to look for in a good rhododendron hybrid. From a nurseryman's perspective a new hybrid should be easy to propagate, disease free and produce flowers in its second year, preferably from its first. Jeff referred to American hybridist Ted Van Veen who had a comprehensive list of criteria for new hybrids. *R.* 'Cunningham's White' has been used in hybridising for its good disease resistance, while *R. yakushimanum* is used for its good foliage retention. Jeff's 'Kiwi' series is a result of complex and deliberate crosses using F1 *R. yakushimanum* hybrids.

Jeff gave me a demonstration of hybridising rhododendrons from stripping off the petals of the pollen donor, and transferring the pollen to the stigma of the seed parent whose stamens had been removed. He also showed me other aspects of running a nursery. He described how a tornado came through the nursery destroying some of the glasshouses and polytunnels. It proved to be a blessing in disguise in that it made them change the way they do things. They found that taking bigger cuttings produced bigger and better plants sooner than conventional cuttings. An employee also accidentally changed the mist setting to sprinkler. This turned out to be better too. A sprinkler gives 91% uniformity whereas mist tends to move. The sprinklers also removed the need for hand watering. My visit to Elliotts Nursery proved to be one of the most educational experiences of my trip.

A lot of breeding work has been carried out at Dunedin. McKenzie (1985) gives a detailed account of how the Rhododendron Dell at Dunedin Botanic Garden was developed by David Tannock. He was appointed Superintendent of Reserves in 1903 and continued to develop the gardens until 1940, introducing many rhododendron species during this time. Some were imported from the UK including from the Royal Botanic Gardens Kew. Others were from plant hunting expeditions such as from Joseph Rock in China and Tibet (Cameron 1986, cited in Coker and Millar, 1998). As a collection of rhododendrons, it was unmatched in New Zealand during this period. The climate and soil of Dunedin seems to enable rhododendrons to prosper, hence the achievements of David Tannock and his successors.

Maurice Skipworth took over from David Tannock in 1940 and continued to improve the gardens until 1967. Balch (1975) describes the detailed hybridisation work carried out at Dunedin Botanic Garden during this time, which included making crosses which had

RHODODENDRON 'ROBERT BALCH'   **WILLIAM STANGER**

not been previously trialled, thus avoiding repetition of what had already been tried. Balch also describes how the parent plants were chosen for their merits which would be passed on to their progeny. Hybrids from this era include *Rhododendron* 'Lovelock', 'Alpine Meadow' and 'Robert Balch'. 'Robert Balch' (*arboreum* ssp. *zeylanicum* × *elliottii* KW 19083) has rich red flowers with darker spotting in the throat, and glossy green leaves. It prefers partial shade, but is wind tolerant. 'Alpine Meadow' (a selection from seedlings of *R. leucaspis*) has white flowers, but is slightly tender and only grows to 60cm after 10 years, being wider than it is high and forming a tidy, compact plant with attractive scaly foliage.

My short stint at the Rhododendron Dell was spent helping the current curator Doug Thomson. The main focus was fine-tuning the garden ready for an assessment by the New Zealand Garden Trust. The pressure was on to maintain the Botanic Garden's 6-star international status. Whist laying siege to the dreaded *Tropaeolum speciosum,* I was given my initial introduction to New Zealand rhododendrons. The native bush is always regenerating, and consequently needs managing so it enhances the rhododendron collection rather than overpowering it. Sometimes a grubber or mattock is needed to dig out larger saplings. The Rhododendron Dell is about 10 acres and is looked after by Doug and an apprentice, and there is always plenty to do. The collection of species rhododendrons is arranged into the subsections of the genus. However, over time Doug has found it increasingly difficult to stick to this plan due to lack of space. Doug also gave me an insight into his and New Zealand's involvement in *ex situ* conservation of *Rhododendron* species.

Both Doug Thompson (2017) and Dr Marion MacKay (2017) go into great detail describing New Zealand's approach to *Rhododendron* conservation and how the initial data collection of plants growing in the country was undertaken.

In 2015, The Pukeiti Rhododendron Trust committed to increase its collection of wild source Red List species to enrich and promote the Pukeiti Rhododendron Collection as an *ex situ* conservation collection, as part of a National Conservation Plan for Rhododendron Species. Part of the plan is to assess the range of rhododendron species within New Zealand and to identify which are endangered. Rare species are propagated and distributed to other parts of the country where they are thought to grow best. Seed collection in the wild is supported by this initiative to increase the range of provenance of rare or endangered species already in New Zealand. Because of strict biosecurity measures in New Zealand, no new species (those that have no record of being in NZ) can be introduced to the country. It is also worth bearing in mind that the Southern Hemisphere has different clones of rhododendron species to those in the Northern Hemisphere. In order to gather data on what rhododendron species are present in New Zealand, a verifier for both North and South Islands visits gardens to ensure plants are true to type. Doug Thompson is the verifier for the South, while Sue Davies is responsible for the North. The data is fed back to Marion Mackay to process and compare with other international collections and thus establish how the New Zealand collection may best support and collaborate with rhododendron species conservation internationally.

New Zealand is home to one of the most significant species rhododendron collections in the world. The story of Pukeiti at Taranaki is well documented by Pat Greenfield (1997) and she describes how (William) Douglas Cook could not grow rhododendrons at his own property at Eastwoodhill. Along with Russell Matthews, Douglas investigated Pukeiti after being prompted by Ernie Alderman MP and Arthur Goudie. One visit was enough and he bought the site. The land was offered to the NZRA but they declined, and this led to the formation of The Pukeiti Rhododendron Trust in 1951. Pukeiti sits at an elevation of 520 metres. Being within regenerating rainforest, it has a high rainfall of 3–4m annually, which the rhododendrons enjoy to a degree, but drainage in places leaves much to be desired. The climatic conditions allow the big leaf rhododendrons to grow unhindered and many are happily self-seeding. To find out what these hybrids were, the then curator, Graham Smith, made deliberate crosses to give some indication of what the self-set hybrids could be.

At the same time, a small selection of these deliberate hybrids was named: 'Jack Anderson', 'Ina Hair', 'Gordon Collier', 'Geoff Broker' and 'Barbara Hayes'. These are covered in the wonderful volume *Big-leaf Rhododendrons: Growing the giants of the genus* written by the authoritative Kiwi horticulturists Glyn Church and Graham Smith (2015). 'Barbara Hayes' (*hodgsonii* × *grande*) is my favourite big leaf hybrid, and I was at Pukeiti when it put on its best ever performance according to Graham Smith. It was a good year in general to see the big leaf rhododendrons in flower. 'Barbara Hayes' has marvellous pink flowers with a crenulated edge to the corolla, the pink fades to cream and various stages of this colour transition are apparent on a plant in full bloom. The silver indumentum on the back of the leaves further enhances the overall display. The original seed was brought back from a plant found by Des Hayes on a steep bank in Sikkim, northeast India. It was originally thought to be *Rhododendron grande* but its appearance and original location fits perfectly between *R. grande* and *R. hodgsonii*.

My own contribution to Pukeiti largely consisted of creating vistas to show off the magnificent floral beasts of rhododendrons resplendent in the rainforest. Much bushwhacking was carried out to give

RHODODENDRON 'BARBARA HAYES'   WILLIAM STANGER

NEW VISTA TO SHOW OFF THE RHODODENDRONS AT PUKEITI   **WILLIAM STANGER**

best gardens in the world to see these truly mesmerising plants. It is also home to an impressive collection of vireya rhododendrons. They are mostly grown under a covered walkway with open sides, so consequently they look a lot better than pot specimens grown in a glasshouse. Further north around the Auckland area, vireyas grow happily outside.

It is not possible to write about New Zealand hybrid rhododendrons without mentioning its most famous contribution, *R.* 'Rubicon'. Graham Smith told a group of us at Pukeiti how Ron Gordon sowed seed of 'Noyo Chief' × 'Kilimanjaro'. 'Rubicon' was effectively the runt of the litter but Gordon thought it was worth persevering with. He potted it on, planted it in the garden and it has become one of the world's most sought-after red rhododendrons. The cardinal red flowers are spotted black inside the upper lobes, forming a compact truss on a compact plant, with wonderful dark and glossy foliage. One of Ron's mother's favourite sayings was 'crossing the Rubicon' referring to the name of the stream that Caesar crossed before waging war with Pompey. It has come to mean a boundary which once passed, means one is committed. 'Committed' definitely describes Ron Gordon along with many other rhododendron hybridists.

the rhododendrons breathing space. It was suggested that I carry out a legacy project, so I worked on the Graham Smith and Richardson Walks, opening up vistas to show off the rhododendrons. I also helped plant drifts of azaleas at the beginning of Richardson Walk leading to the Valley of the Giants. There are big plans to further enhance what could be said to be the most dynamic garden in New Zealand. As well as the management of the garden and its plants, the Head Gardener Andrew Brooker told me about the conservation of New Zealand hybrids, and elaborated on their assessment. It has been suggested that a trial be undertaken with trial beds at various locations in the country, but Andrew would argue that more than sufficient knowledge is already held by the nursery people and gardeners who already grow these plants, such as Woodbury Rhododendrons and Cross Hills Nursery. These highly informed individuals can tell you what will grow well in each area, which hybrids are the star performers, and how to get the best out of them. Bailey and Millar (2013) described the prior efforts of conservation for New Zealand hybrids and earlier trials which have come to an end.

Pukeiti is able to grow early flowering big leaf species that are a challenge in the UK. Both *R. magnificum* and particularly *R. protistum* are well represented. I was thrilled to see *R. protistum* 'Pukeiti' in full flower. Pukeiti is certainly one of the

RHODODENDRON PROTISTUM 'PUKEITI'   **WILLIAM STANGER**

Andrew Brooker conducted a survey to determine which New Zealand rhododendron hybrids are most favoured by Kiwis (the people not the bird!). Favourites include 'Floral Dance', 'Rubicon', 'Lemon Lodge', 'Van Dec', 'Stead's Best', 'Mary Tasker', 'Petticoat Lane', 'Spiced Honey', 'Beverley Tasker', 'Bonnie Doone', 'Carla Van Zon', 'Kotuku', 'Sir Edmund Hillary', 'Mollie Coker', 'Mrs George Huthnance', 'Alpine Meadow' and 'Kiwi Pearl'. I do not know how all of these perform elsewhere in the world. Andrew Brooker said that 'Lemon Lodge' although fine in New Zealand

WORKING BEE AT PUKEITI. GARDENERS FROM PUKEITI, TUPARE AND HOLLARD GARDENS, WITH WILLIAM STANGER AT CENTRE **WILLIAM STANGER**

can suffer from leaf spot in the UK when subjected to stressful conditions. *Crossing The Rubicon: New Zealand Raised Rhododendrons, A Handbook* (Coker and Millar, 1998) provides information on all New Zealand hybrids up to 1998.

There are many more Kiwis who have hybridised rhododendrons, but I'll conclude with the Jurys at Tikorangi Garden, near Taranaki. Abbie Jury (2011) gives a thorough account of 'The Jury Rhododendron Legacy'. Her father-in-law Felix Jury, tried to address some of the issues associated with growing rhododendrons in some of New Zealand's more challenging areas. Abbie told me how in parts of

RHODODENDRON 'STEAD'S BEST' **WILLIAM STANGER**

the North Island there is a lack of a winter chill, which means that some rhododendrons and many other plants survive but don't perform as well as one would like. This also means that devastating thrips stay alive and turn rhododendron foliage silver. The intense light of New Zealand can also burn both foliage and flowers. To this end, Felix Jury used *R. polyandrum* which has passed on its superb resistance to thrips and leaf burn to its offspring. Of these *R.* 'Moon Orchid' (*polyandrum* × 'Sirius') is considered the most garden worthy. The scented flowers are held in a loose truss and are frilly edged, apricot and yellow. The other one to go for is 'Felicity Fair', combining good foliage with fragrant flowers in creamy yellow, suffused pink on the outside of the throat.

New Zealand, annoyingly for the rest of us, has no issue with growing rhododendrons of the Maddenia subsection. Consequently, Kiwis have bred a number of interesting hybrids: The Jurys' 'Floral Dance' has glossy bullate foliage, with white flushed camellia-rose flowers possessing a yellow blotch in the throat; the lobes are very frilled. It combines the best characteristics of its parents (*nuttallii* × *edgeworthii*). 'Floral Gift' ('Michael's Pride' × *polyandrum*) has a sturdy habit of growth, with healthy foliage on a compact plant. The highly fragrant and textured

RHODODENDRON 'SOFT LIGHTS' (*TOP LEFT*); *R.* 'MOON ORCHID' (*TOP RIGHT*)
RHODODENDRON 'ILAM CREAM' (*CENTRE LEFT*); *R.* 'KIWI MAGIC' (*CENTRE RIGHT*)
RHODODENDRON 'MOLLIE COKER' (*BOTTOM LEFT*) *R.* 'ILAM CARMEN' (*BOTTOM RIGHT*)

WILLIAM STANGER

MAGNOLIA 'FELIX JURY'   **WILLIAM STANGER**

MAGNOLIA 'HONEY TULIP'   **WILLIAM STANGER**

flowers are weather resistant, and are white with a yellow throat, bearing a hint of pink on the petal backs.

The Jurys however are mostly known for their magnolias. Abbie (Jury, 2017) tells the story of the Jury Magnolias and highlights the selections they have named. She has likewise done the same for their camellias (Jury, 2014) and vireyas (2012). Felix Jury started hybridising with *Magnolia* 'Mark Jury', named after his son. It was meant to be *Magnolia campbellii* ssp. *mollicomata* 'Lanarth' but is probably a hybrid of 'Lanarth' × *sargentiana*. From 'Mark Jury' as a pollen donor, Felix bred five named cultivars. He also named three more unrelated hybrids. The Jurys rate 'Iolanthe' as one of the best that Felix named. As the original plant has matured the flowers have stayed large. It also sets flower buds down the stem, prolonging the bloom period for up to two months.

Magnolia 'Vulcan' in its day represented a colour breakthrough and set the standard for future red cultivars. It looks spectacular in New Zealand but in colder climates has yet to prove itself. Vaughan Gallavan (2016) gives an overview of red-flowered magnolias and the issues of 'Vulcan' in the UK. Mark Jury has named and released four magnolias, with two or three more in the pipeline. His 'Felix Jury' is a star performer, and its large deep pink flowers improve with age every year. The lovely red colouration of the buds when opening, persists at the base of the tepals. Good specimens can be seen at The Garden House (Devon) and RHS Wisley.

More recently Mark released 'Honey Tulip' and I saw the original plant in flower at Tikorangi. It has heavy textured weather-resistant petals, held in a solid cup form. It also has the advantage of flowering well in advance of the emerging foliage, and the Jurys report a generous bud set.

Ian Baldick (2009) another New Zealand magnolia breeder outlines the history of *Magnolia campbellii* in New Zealand. The first known introduction of *M. campbellii* to New Zealand was around 1850–60s via Thomas Mason. He contributed to Himalayan seed gathering expeditions and presumably received seed of *M. campbellii* collected in the wild. This was later known as the 'Mason Form' and was the first *M. campbellii* to flower in New Zealand. In the 1950s Duncan and Davies was the largest propagation nursery in New Zealand, and during this time they imported other forms of *M. campbellii* from British gardens such as the Caerhays form of *M. campbellii* ssp. *mollicomata* and other forms from Hillier Nurseries. In the 1980s Peter Cave extended the range with more imported cultivars such as 'Darjeeling' and 'Kew's Surprise', and in the early 1990s the nursery brought in 'Betty Jessel' and 'Wakehurst' among others.

Another notable magnolia breeder is Vance Hooper of Magnolia Grove, also near Taranaki. He describes his work and named selections in a couple of articles (Hooper, 2010 and 2018). The main focus of Vance's hybridising programme is to achieve more compact plants for the ever-shrinking domestic garden. He also highlights, like many other professional breeders, that only a small handful of plants actually get named from hundreds if not thousands of plants raised. Knowing how particular such breeders are in their selection of new releases gives you more confidence that you are acquiring something distinctly unique and garden worthy.

Perhaps the most well know and deservedly popular of Vance's hybrids are *Magnolia* 'Genie' and 'Margaret Helen'. 'Genie' is truly compact and upright with rich red flowers. These flowers may not be the largest but are borne in profusion. 'Margaret Helen' is similar to 'Caerhays Surprise' but possesses a brighter reddish-pink tone that shines out even on the dullest day. I have got my eye on 'Ice Queen', which has only just been released. Effectively it is a white *M. campbellii* but is easier to grow than the species, being free-flowering with a hardy constitution. It combines the best of its parents 'Cameo' × *M. campbellii* 'Mount Pirongia'. There are more exciting hybrids that are yet to be released.

Vance has created a useful reference collection of New Zealand selected magnolias. I was lucky to make a couple of visits and be guided around the garden by Vance while they were in flower, so consequently I took numerous photographs. There are many to choose from but the following few

MAGNOLIA 'AURORA'   **WILLIAM STANGER**

caught my eye in particular. 'Strawberry Fields' ('Spectrum' × 'Vulcan') was bred by Ian Baldick. The flowers are bright strawberry red arising from a strong growing upright tree. 'Aurora' was raised by Os Blumhardt at Whangarei, and is considered one of his best hybrids. It is a cross between 'Star Wars' and *M. sargentiana* var. *robusta*. It forms a columnar tree with an upright habit and commences flowering in its second or third year from planting. Vance has noticed at Magnolia Grove that 'Aurora' will flower like clockwork every year while other varieties are less consistent and seem affected by the weather. 'Purple Sensation', another Ian Baldick hybrid, is reminiscent of one of its parents 'Lanarth'. It is thus a good alternative for 'Lanarth' with an upright habit and will flower within 3–4 years from planting with sumptuous purple flowers. A number of magnolia hybrids from the subsection *Michelia* have been bred in New Zealand. *Magnolia doltsopa* 'Silver Cloud' was selected by Duncan and Davis in the 1950–60s; it layered better than the other forms by setting flower buds on the first year layers. 'Snow Dove' (*maudiae* × *doltsopa*) is a hybrid that arose as a rootstock seedling at Auckland Botanic Gardens, and has a wonderful sweet and spicy aroma, with ice white, perfectly formed blooms. Oswald Blumhardt hybridised *M. doltsopa* 'Silver Cloud' and *M. figo* to produce 'Mixed Up Miss' and 'Bubbles'. Mark Jury started hybridising plants within the subsection *Michelia* in the 1990s. The resultant hybrids that have been named are sold under the Fairy Magnolia brand as Fairy Magnolia 'Blush', 'Cream' and 'White'.

MAGNOLIA GROVE: VANCE HOOPER AND WILLIAM STANGER (*LEFT*) WITH *M*. 'GENIE'   **WILLIAM STANGER**

Vonnie Cave (1998) provides an overview of New Zealand raised camellias. However, I will focus on the smaller flowered varieties that are being selected for resistance to the notorious camellia petal blight, from which New Zealand camellias suffer greatly. Auckland Botanic Garden has a breeding programme to combat petal blight, and is using *Camellia* 'Transluscent' (*transnokoensis* × *lutchuensis*), whose species parents are both petal blight resistant. It should be noted that some supposedly resistant selections are in fact not resistant but avoid petal blight by flowering early in the season. The small flowers show less of the symptoms and are quickly replaced by successive blooms. Extensive research has been carried out on the resistance of camellias to camellia petal blight, a prime example being Taylor (2004).

The resistant species also seem resistant to setting seed and it is proving difficult to pass on petal blight resistant genes to the next generation. Mark Jury told me that *Camellia lutchuensis* is particularly un-cooperative at bearing seed. It is consequently used as a pollen parent which evidently means those resistant genes are not being passed on. However, he was fortunate to find a seed-bearing specimen which gave rise to 'Fairy Blush' and a very fine plant it is too. It is an upright grower with buds that are deep pink on the outside, opening to look like apple blossoms of about 5cm wide. It looked very impressive as a hedge at the Jury's garden. Other petal blight resistant selections are 'Transpink', 'Festival of Lights', 'Sweet Jane', 'Wirlinga Bride' and 'Spring Festival'. The flowers are generally smaller than the average camellia hybrid, but are larger than the parent species. Their more natural appearance appeals to more contemporary tastes. As a bonus the *C. lutchuensis* hybrids have inherited some of their parent's fragrance. The next step is to backcross with *C. lutchuensis,* in the hope that the resistant genes are passed on.

Rhododendrons, camellias and magnolias are all well represented in New Zealand and, although a young country, it is building up a rich horticultural heritage. The breeding work has given the world many wonderful new plants to adorn its gardens. New Zealand is home to many knowledgeable plantspeople whom I had the pleasure of meeting during my travels. I can assure you, it is worth the long journey to the other side of the world.

MAGNOLIA 'STRAWBERRY FIELDS'   WILLIAM STANGER

MAGNOLIA 'ICE QUEEN'   WILLIAM STANGER

MAGNOLIA 'PURPLE SENSATION'   WILLIAM STANGER

CAMELLIA 'SWEET JANE'   **WILLIAM STANGER**

ACKNOWLEDGEMENTS

I would like to thank the Rhododendron, Camellia and Magnolia Group, the RHS Coke Trust Bursary Fund, the RHS Jimmy Smart Bursary Fund, the Merlin Trust, the Hardy Plant Society (Kenneth Black Bursary) and the Devon Group of Plant Heritage, for their sponsorship which contributed to a year's study trip in New Zealand. My appreciation goes to all those who have supported me both before and during my travels in New Zealand.

REFERENCES

Balch, R. (1975) 'Hybridising Rhododendrons at the Dunedin Botanic Gardens', *Dunedin Rhododendron Group Bulletin*, 3.

Baldick, I. (2009) 'A history of *Magnolia campbellii* in New Zealand', *Rhododendrons, Camellias and Magnolias (RHS)*, 60.

Bailey, G. and Millar, K. (2013) 'Beyond the Rubicon: conservation of New Zealand rhododendron hybrids', *Rhododendrons, Camellias and Magnolias (RHS)*, 73.

Cave, V. (1998) 'Raised in New Zealand', *Rhododendrons with Camellias and Magnolias (RHS)*, 49.

Church, G. and Smith, G. (2015) *Big-leaf Rhododendrons: Growing the Giants of the Genus*. Auckland: David Bateman Ltd.

Coker, B. and Millar, K (1998) *Crossing the Rubicon: New Zealand Raised Rhododendrons, A Handbook*. Canterbury: Canterbury Rhododendron Society Inc.

Coker, B. (2017) 'The Legacy of Mollie and Ron Coker of Ilam, Christchurch', *The New Zealand Rhododendron*, 5.

Gallavan, V. (2016) 'Red-flowered magnolias' *The Plantsman, (RHS)*, [www document] https://www.rhs.org.uk/about-the-rhs/publications/magazines/the-plantsman/2016-Issues/March/TP-Mar16-Magnolia-red.pdf (accessed 04. December. 2018).

Greenfield, P. (1997) *Pukeiti: New Zealand's Finest Rhododendron Garden*. Auckland: David Bateman Ltd.

Hooper, V. (2010) 'Harnessing the wheel of experience: intelligent magnolia hybridisation', *Rhododendrons, Camellias and Magnolias (RHS)*, 61.

Hooper, V. (2018) 'A Lifetime of Hybridising Magnolias', *Rhododendrons, Camellias and Magnolias (RHS)*, 69.

Jury, A. (2011) 'The Jury Rhododendron Legacy', *Rhododendrons, Camellias and Magnolias (RHS)*, 62.

Jury, A. (2012) 'The Jury Vireya Legacy', *Rhododendrons, Camellias and Magnolias (RHS)*, 63.

Jury, A. (2014) 'The Jury Camellia Legacy', *Rhododendrons, Camellias and Magnolias (RHS)*, 65.

Jury, A. (2017) 'The Jury Magnolia Legacy', *Rhododendrons, Camellias and Magnolias (RHS)*, 68.

Dr MacKay, M. (2017) 'Development of a New Zealand Ex-Situ Conservation Strategy for Rhododendrons, Project Report to the end of June 2017', *The New Zealand Rhododendron*, 5.

Dr MacKay, M. (2017) 'Uncommon Rhododendron Species in New Zealand: Are there any at the bottom of your garden?', *The New Zealand Rhododendron*, 5.

McKenzie, B. (1985) 'The Rhododendron Dell, Dunedin Botanic Garden; Some early history', *Dunedin Rhododendron Group Bulletin*, 13.

Millar, K. (2015) 'Ilam: the creation of Edgar Fraser Stead', *New Zealand Rhododendron Association Bulletin*.

Millar, K. and Morten, R. (ed.) (2005) 'Yours Sincerely F Kingdon-Ward', *New Zealand Rhododendron Association Bulletin*, 93.

Millar, K. and Morten, R. (ed.) (2003) 'New Zealand Plant Hunters', *New Zealand Rhododendron Association Bulletin*, 91.

Dr Salinger, J. (1994) 'In Memoriam: Dr John Yeates', *The New Zealand Rhododendron Association. 50th Jubilee 1944–1994*.

Stead, E. (1947) 'Rhododendrons in New Zealand', *The Rhododendron Year Book (RHS)*.

Taylor, C. (2004) *Studies of Camellia Flower Blight (Ciborinia camelliae KOHN)* [www document] https://muir.massey.ac.nz/bitstream/handle/10179/1722/02_whole.pdf (accessed 13. September. 2018).

WILLIAM STANGER

is a keen young horticulturist with a love of rhododendrons, camellias and magnolias, who was a recipient of a grant from the RCMG to help with his travel to New Zealand.

Combating Camellia Petal Blight: Can Modern Biology Help Our Camellias?

CAMELLIA PETAL BLIGHT

This blight is caused by the fungus *Ciborinia camelliae* and is a problem of international scale. The fungus is believed to have originated in East Asia, and it spread rapidly all over the world in the second half of the 20th century, even reaching remote New Zealand in 1993. The disease is caused by the growth of fungal mycelium within camellia petal tissues. Growth starts with the germination of fungal spores that have landed on the petal surface (*see the figure below*). The mycelium enters the petal and can completely engulf the bloom within days. After the blooms fall onto the soil, so-called sclerotia then form at the base of infected blooms. The fungus will stay dormant until climate conditions induce the

growth of a fruiting body, which can produce millions of spores. Spores are easily carried by wind for great distances and this, together with the sheer number of spores, makes the control of the disease incredibly challenging. The approaches used to treat the disease can be classified into two major groups: killing of the fungus or making plants resistant to the infection. Here we summarize research, conducted by teams from Italy, Spain and New Zealand, that aims to find ways to combat the disease.

KNOW YOUR ENEMY

Prof Marco Saracchi and his team from the University of Milan in Italy aim to better understand our fungal enemy, with the purpose

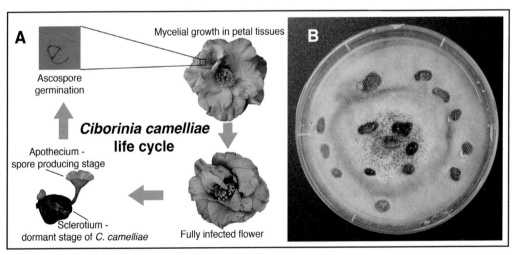

(A) LIFECYCLE OF *CIBORINA CAMELLIAE*, WHICH CAUSES PETAL BLIGHT. THE INFECTION STARTS FROM THE ASCOSPORE LANDING ON THE PETAL SURFACE. AFTER GERMINATION, MYCELIUM GROWS INSIDE PETAL TISSUE, CAUSING BROWNING AND PREMATURE FALL OF THE BLOOM. FALLEN BLOOMS ALLOW THE FORMATION OF SCLEROTIA, THE DORMANT STAGE OF THE FUNGUS. FRUITING BODIES (APOTHECIA) GROW FROM SCLEROTIA AND RELEASE NEW SPORES, REPEATING THE CYCLE (B) MYCELIAL STAGE OF THE FUNGUS, WHICH GROWS INSIDE PETAL TISSUES, CAN ALSO BE GROWN IN LAB DISHES FOR RESEARCH.

(A) FIELD STUDIES OF FUNGAL VIABILITY
(B) MICROPHOTOGRAPH OF THE SPORES SITTING IN FRUITING BODIES
(C) RELEASED FUNGAL SPORES STAINED WITH SPECIAL GREEN FLUORESCENT DYE

of finding their weaknesses. They collected about 200 *C. camelliae* strains from different regions within Italy and other countries. They study population variability from a phenotypic and genotypic point of view in order to understand how the fungus has adapted to the variety of climatic conditions present around the globe. Marco and his group also study the different stages of fungal lifecycle and measure the viability of spores and sclerotia. One of the approaches to combat the disease involves the application of fungicides and biocontrol agents to reduce the fungal viability in field conditions. Sclerotia are the dormant stage of the fungus and are highly resistant to anti-fungal treatments, thanks to their thick and strong rind. However, some other microorganisms are able to attack and kill this dormant stage. Thus biocontrol of the dormant stage and fungicides that attack the growing, non-dormant, stage of the fungus may be the most effective way to control the fungus.

HOW DOES THE FUNGUS KILL PETALS?

The New Zealand group, led by Associate Prof. Paul Dijkwel at Massey University, studies how the fungus kills plant cells. All pathogens release numerous compounds to suppress host resistance and to kill and digest cells. Knowledge about these fungal weapons allows for the development of a defence strategy. Among the most popular fungal weapons are specific proteins and the New Zealand group have discovered that the camellia parasite can produce toxic proteins that may cause the browning and fall of the blooms. They have extracted fungal proteins from infected blooms and found dozens of proteins including those that can destroy plant cell walls, digest plant proteins and disrupt normal antioxidant levels in the tissues. The team has been able to synthesise the fungal

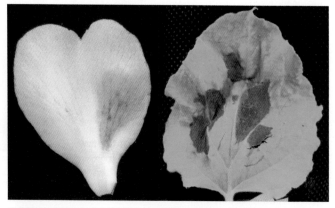

INJECTION OF TOXIC FUNGAL WEAPON-PROTEINS CAUSES CELL DEATH IN *CAMELLIA* 'NICKY CRISP' PETAL (*LEFT*) AND MODEL-PLANT *NICOTIANA BENTHAMIANA* LEAF (*RIGHT*)

HIGHLY-SUSCEPTIBLE *CAMELLIA* 'NICKY CRISP' (*LEFT*) AND RESISTANT *CAMELLIA LUTCHUENSIS* (*RIGHT*) PLANTS FROM MASSEY UNIVERSITY, NEW ZEALAND

proteins in the lab to study which particular parts of plant cells the *C. camelliae* weapon-proteins are targeting and which of these are the most important ones for the fungus. Interestingly, fungal weapon-proteins were found to be harmful not only to camellias but also to other plants, which makes it possible to study them even without a constant supply of the petals. These proteins trigger death of plant cells, being toxic, and also cause cell lysis creating a comfortable environment for *C. camelliae* to grow.

NATURALLY RESISTANT CAMELLIA PLANTS

There is a disease control method gifted to us by nature itself: some camellia plants cannot be easily defeated by petal blight. A study conducted by the New Zealand group, together with Daniel Charvet from the USA demonstrated that different *Camellia* species and hybrids vary considerably in their resistance to petal blight. Using a spore-based resistance testing system, *Camellia lutchuensis* and *C. transnokoensis*

were found to be highly resistant species, while a hybrid of *Camellia japonica* and *Camellia pitardii* var. *pitardii*, (*Camellia* 'Nicky Crisp'), was found to be extremely susceptible. The Spanish research team made similar observations and added *C. longicarpa* to the list of resistant species. These findings fuel a new page in the history of the research on petal blight resistance. Current and new projects in New Zealand and Spain aim to investigate the mechanisms of resistance on the level of molecules and genes.

HOW DO RESISTANT PLANTS DEFEND THEMSELVES?

There is no area in science that did not benefit from the rapid development of computational technologies, and plant biology is certainly not an exception. Plants, including our favourite camellias, store huge amounts of genetic data in their cells, and we are now able to read, understand and analyse this type of big biological data. The New Zealand team obtained blueprints of all proteins from *C. lutchuensis* and *Camellia* 'Nicky Crisp'. Proteins are molecules that perform almost all functions in living organisms and to understand the mechanisms of disease resistance in *C. lutchuensis*, the team determined when the production of plant proteins is being switched on and off in response to the fungal attack. They found that the response of the resistant plant to the fungus is fast and furious. Resistant plant cells very quickly recognize the fungal attack and start to produce many resistance proteins within hours, and this causes the production of compounds that limit the growth of the fungus. Susceptible 'Nicky Crisp' plant cells, on the other hand, do not seem to recognize the fungal invader until it is too late. While it is

DEVELOPMENT OF A NEW CAMELLIA PLANT FROM A CELL CULTURE OF *C. JAPONICA*. THIS LABORATORY TECHNIQUE ALLOWS CAMELLIA PLANTS TO OBTAIN NEW TRAITS

– as of yet – unclear why the susceptible hybrid fails to detect the fungus, the research has identified two possible approaches to control the disease in our gardens: the New Zealand team is currently testing hormonal treatments that can boost the plant immune system, making it uncomfortable for the fungus to establish and grow. Secondly, the team aims to control the disease by spraying susceptible blooms with the fungal growth-limiting compounds that resistant plants produce naturally.

RESISTANCE BREEDING ASSISTED BY MOLECULAR BIOLOGY

We cannot yet point to the single trait that gives the power of resistance to *C. lutchuensis*. Petal-blight resistance is a complex process involving multiple proteins doing their job in the right place and at the right time. The next step would be to identify the most important resistance proteins and determine how these resistance proteins behave in hybrids of resistant and susceptible plants. Having a big pool of various *Camellia* hybrids with known parentage is crucial for such future studies, and the

involvement of camellia researchers and enthusiasts from all over the world is needed. First of all, we would like to encourage people to breed new hybrids of resistant *C. lutchuensis*, *C. transnokoensis* and *C. longicarpa* with susceptible plants. We would like to mention here two fantastic projects aiming to breed petal blight-resistant hybrids with great-looking blooms. Neville Haydon initiated an influential petal-blight resistance breeding movement in New Zealand: Auckland Botanic Gardens together with the Auckland Branch of the New Zealand Camellia Society established the *Neville Haydon Award* and currently support new generations of breeders. You can read more about this project here (https://bit.ly/2P8JOoG). Daniel and Patty Charvet from the USA (Fort Bragg, California) every year hand-pollinate their flowers and have obtained already hundreds of hybrids useful for resistance studies (https://bit.ly/2BCC4wz). No doubt there will be other activities in different countries that we have not yet heard about. In addition to breeding resistance, these projects may give us blooms with exciting new combinations of colour shape and fragrance.

GENETIC IMPROVEMENT CAN MAKE SUSCEPTIBLE HYBRIDS RESISTANT

The Spanish team includes researchers from the Plant Pathology Station of Areeiro (Pontevedra) and the University of Vigo. Their efforts are focused on the genetic improvement of the *Camellia* genus, with a specific interest in *Camellia japonica*. They first developed a laboratory-based biological model to complement field studies carried out with infected flowers. Using their model system, the group was able to complete the lifecycle of the fungus – for the first time as far as we know. The model will prove very useful in research as it allows experiments to be performed throughout the year, independent of the petal blight season.

Further development of the model is expected to allow the team to genetically modify *Camellia* plants. Genetic modification is a technique that can add traits to the genetic makeup of a plant. However, in some parts of the world – notably in Europe and New Zealand – the growth of genetically modified plants in our gardens is regulated by strict rules. Thus, while this work is still at an early stage of development, the prospect of making our current favourite camellia hybrids resistant is an enticing one.

FUTURE PERSPECTIVES.

While past experience and research has taught us that there is no easy way to defeat the fungus, our research provides a way forward. By studying the fungus, we are discovering the fungus' weaknesses and strengths. Dissecting the resistance response has provided important clues of why some plants are resistant and others are not. The ability to study the disease in controlled laboratory conditions and make genetically modified camellia plants will allow us to test hypotheses and might allow us to make current susceptible hybrids resistant. We are working towards the creation of new resistant hybrids and cultivars and do not give up on our susceptible plants. We are aiming to improve the biocontrol methods in order to protect *Camellia* collections present in our gardens and parks.

In addition, all camellia lovers can help! We would like to encourage you to cross *C. lutchuensis*, *C. transnokoensis*, and *C. longicarpa*, – currently not the most popular plants among breeders – with susceptible plants to create new hybrids. Multiple crosses with resistant species may be required to obtain sufficient resistance to petal blight, but the results will no doubt create hybrids with exciting bloom qualities. Since the fungus propagates easily and rapidly, it is essential that any local procedures to limit fungal spores be applied systematically and in big territories. Even one forgotten shrub can be the source of infection of a huge area.

The petal blight problem will likely require a multipronged approach including the development of resistant hybrids and the use of chemical, biological and agronomical control methods. We believe that widely supported international collaboration is of critical importance to achieve the desirable results. Making publicly available databases of resistant species and hybrids and new ways of communication between camellia breeders sharing their success in the disease control will take us even closer to solving the petal blight problem. These systematic measures should help us reduce the petal blight problem to the scale of a typical seasonal influenza, instead of medieval plague or smallpox outbreaks.

ACKNOWLEDGEMENTS.

First of all the authors would like to thank all the members of their research teams. The studies described here would not be possible without the involvement of the international camellia community. We would like to thank the Spanish Camellia Society, and President Carmen Salinero, the Italian Camellia Society, the Swiss Camellia Society, the New Zealand Camellia Society, the Camellia Memorial Trust, and Tony Barnes for their support and guidance of our research.

NIKOLAI KONDRATEV
is based at the Institute of Fundamental Sciences, Massey University, Palmerston North, New Zealand

MARCO SARACCHI
is based at DeFENS: The Department of Food, Environmental and Nutritional Sciences, University of Milan, Italy

JOSE LUIS COUSELO
is based at the Department of Plant Biology and Soil Science, University of Vigo, Spain

PAUL DIJKWEL
is based at the Institute of Fundamental Sciences, Massey University, Palmerston North, New Zealand

The Magnolia Collection at the JC Raulston Arboretum, North Carolina State University

The JC Raulston Arboretum (JCRA) is a nationally acclaimed garden with one of the most diverse collections of cold hardy temperate zone plants in the southeastern United States. As a part of the Department of Horticultural Science at North Carolina State University in Raleigh, NC, the JCRA is primarily a working research and teaching garden that focuses on the evaluation, selection and display of plant material gathered from around the world and planted in landscape settings. Plants especially adapted to Piedmont North Carolina conditions are identified in an effort to increase the diversity in

THE JC RAULSTON ARBORETUM ENTRANCE
MARK WEATHINGTON & JC RAULSTON ARBORETUM

southern US landscapes. The JCRA's 4.25 hectares and nursery contain over 12,000 accessions of over 7500 different taxa.

The JCRA was named for its founder, Dr J. C. Raulston who started the Arboretum in 1976. J. C. was a tireless plant evangelist dedicated to "diversifying the American landscape." J. C. and his namesake arboretum (renamed from the more prosaic, North Carolina State University Arboretum, after his untimely death in 1996) are well-known for some of the plants released from the JCRA including *Styrax japonicus* 'Emerald Pagoda' and *Calycanthus × raulstonii* 'Hartlage Wine'. In 2004, Horticulture Magazine commissioned a painting titled "A

DR J. C. RAULSTON

MARK WEATHINGTON & JC RAULSTON ARBORETUM

CALYCANTHUS X RAULSTONII 'HARTLAGE WINE'
JOHN MARSTON

Heavenly Garden Party" depicting the 25 most influential deceased gardeners. J. C. Raulston was featured alongside such notables as Capability Brown, Gertrude Jekyll, Graham Stuart Thomas, Rosemary Verey, and Roberto Burle Marx.

Plant introductions from the JCRA continue to influence horticulture. In recent years, the JCRA and Dr Denny Werner have reinvented the butterfly bush, introducing dwarf, functionally sterile selections starting with *Buddleja* 'Blue Chip'. The JCRA redbuds like *Cercis canadensis* 'Ruby Falls' are being grown around the world and the newly released 'Flamethrower' and 'Golden Falls' are game changing advances in the genus.

The Raulston Arboretum's location in the central piedmont of North Carolina allows us to grow a wide diversity of plant material. Our temperatures generally range from about -14°C to 35°C but temperatures much lower and higher are not unknown. The average annual precipitation measures 109cm with most months receiving about 7.5–10cm.

THE MAGNOLIA COLLECTION

Magnolias have been an important part of the collections of the JCRA from its inception. The first accessioned magnolia dates to 1977, less than a year after J. C. Raulston founded the Arboretum. This *Magnolia* × *loebneri* 'Merrill' still graces the Klein-Pringle White Garden where it welcomes the spring with a glorious floral display. The JCRA is a founding member of the American Public Garden Association's multi-institute magnolia collection.

The JCRA's magnolia collection represents a broad diversity of both species and cultivars comprised of 221 individuals of 175 different taxa including 38 species. We currently hold accessions from 9 of the 12 sections of the genus *Magnolia* lacking only taxa in the mostly tropical Talauma, Kmeria, and Manglietiastrum sections. We have a particular focus on members of section Michelia with 33 taxa in this group alone. The complete list of magnolias planted on the grounds of the JCRA can be found on our website (www.ncsu.edu/jcraulstonarboretum) under the "Current Plantings" heading in the "Horticulture" tab. Photographs of many of our magnolias can also be found on the website in the "Photography" section.

The evergreen plants in section Michelia are especially nice since they provide structure and often flowers during our relatively mild winters. *Magnolia ernestii* has made a handsome narrowly upright evergreen tree in the southwest corner of the Japanese Garden where it now towers over the wall. The glossy green leaves are quite attractive and the yellow-white flowers, although not terribly showy, are delightfully fragrant when they appear in late winter to early spring. Our plants (another grows in the Winter Garden) were acquired in 1995 and 1997 and have grown to over 6m in that time. We collected *M. ernestii* var. *szechuanica* on China's famed Emeishan growing happily just below a Buddhist monastery with the *Davidia involucrata* that Ernest Wilson was sent to China to collect.

Another choice plant in this section growing well above the lath house is *M. cavalieri* which

MAGNOLIA MAUDIAE
MARK WEATHINGTON & JC RAULSTON ARBORETUM

MAGNOLIA CAVALIERI VAR. *PLATYPETALA*
MARK WEATHINGTON & JC RAULSTON ARBORETUM

MAGNOLIA AMABILIS

RICHARD FIGLAR

MAGNOLIA COMPRESSA

MARK WEATHINGTON & JC RAULSTON ARBORETUM

begins flowering in December and continues to March. The large, loose white flowers often take winter damage but can be stunning against the clear blue, winter sky. Several clones of *Magnolia maudiae* grace the garden and depending on the selection flower from December through March often with some sporadic flowers throughout the rest of the year. Based on the plants in our collection, there is ample opportunity to select superior forms for the garden.

A recent enigma in the garden is a plant received from Akira Shibamichi of Japan as *M. angustioblonga*. Dick Figlar identified this plant when it came into flower as *M. amabilis*, not to be confused with the *M × soulangeana* cultivar by the same name.

Dick has commented, *"In fall of 2015 I received this plant from Tom* [Ranney] *labeled as M. angustioblonga, which it obviously wasn't! Tom had received the taxon via Brian Upchurch and now I know, thanks to you, that he obtained it from Shibamichi. From the beginning it certainly resembled Sima Yong-Kang's sp. nov.(2006), so I quickly assembled some detailed photos of leaves, stipule scar etc. and sent them on to Sima who confirmed it. He further urged me to check the tepals of the flowers when it blooms, that the tepals should be conspicuously pointed at the tips instead of more less obtuse/rounded to weakly acute or emarginate as in M. laevifolia. Shortly after planting it out in March 2016 the apexes of the tepals confirmed to be acuminate (Sima calls this "contracted-acute at apex" in his paper). ... [H]e fails to mention the most important character for distinguishing M. amabilis from M. laevifolia, which is the 50% long stipular scar on the petiole (as you have aptly observed as well)."*

At any rate, *M. amabilis* appears to form a spreading shrubby plant with narrowly elliptic leaves and fragrant white flowers. The JCRA plant survived over 200 consecutive hours below freezing during the winter of 2018 with little damage but Dick notes that his plant was much more heavily damaged by cold than several other evergreen species.

We have made several collections of *M. compressa*, also in section Michelia, including the doubtfully distinct var. *lanyuensis* from several collecting expeditions to Taiwan since 2009. It is typically found growing with other evergreens in forest settings from low to medium altitudes to around 1800m throughout Taiwan. It is also found in southern Japan and the Phillipines. It makes a large tree to 20m tall with a 1m caliper trunk. Mature specimens are difficult to identify in the wild as the lowest branches can be quite high, especially when growing in the midst of a forested area. The bright red seed coats peeking out from woody capsules on the ground are often the only sign of the tree's presence. The flowers are produced in leaf axils and range in colour from creamy white to pale yellow, typically with a purple base to the tepals and are less than 2cm long. The leaves are usually 5–11cm long, semi-leathery and deep green. It is apparently quite valued in Taiwan as a timber tree. Our collections have been only marginally hardy

MAGNOLIA KACHIRACHIRAI FOLIAGE
MARK WEATHINGTON & JC RAULSTON ARBORETUM

MAGNOLIA LOTUNGENSIS MALE FLOWER
MARK WEATHINGTON & JC RAULSTON ARBORETUM

during our winters. Some of these seedlings come from plants growing at over 2100m in central Taiwan and their lack of hardiness has been surprising. In cultivation in suitable climates, young trees make handsome, narrow, evergreen cones. Unfortunately for a magnolia, the flowers are quite small and tend to be somewhat lost among the foliage. We have distributed these collections widely in the hopes that they will find a more suitable climate in the deeper south and west coast of the U.S.

The other Taiwan magnolia *M. kachirachirai,* a member of section Gynopodium, has proven to be even more elusive. It is endemic to the island, occurring only in very scattered locations near the southern tip at low altitudes to about 1300m. It is another large tree, not quite as tall as *M. compressa*, but with a broader trunk girth. The terminal flowers are 2.5–3.5cm long and pale greenish-yellow. The plant is listed as "endangered" on the 2006 IUCN Red List. According to the Botanic Gardens Conservation International PlantSearch database, there are currently specimens of this plant being cultivated in only 5 other public gardens worldwide.

Armed with location data from colleague Chen Chien-Fan at the Taiwan Forestry Research Institute (TFRI), we set off around the southern tip of Taiwan through a lush landscape in search of *M. kachirachirai*. Despite very accurate GPS and map information, we could not track down the endangered species, although a large, dead tree seemed like a possible candidate for the tree we were seeking. The scattered populations of *M. kachirachirai* make finding it somewhat of a

needle-in-a-haystack situation and we were ultimately forced to abandon the search.

M. lotungensis, also in section Gynopodium has been happily growing in our lath house since 1998 and finally consented to flower a decade later. The creamy cup shaped flowers are quite lovely in April and May but can be difficult to see since they are generally above the roof of the structure. It forms a very distinctive upright, narrow pyramid with new foliage often tinted red on first emerging in the spring. Although it takes many years from seed before flowering, it is an extremely handsome evergreen tree with a uniform habit from my experience. I am told it is

MAGNOLIA DELAVAYI PINK FORM
MARK WEATHINGTON & JC RAULSTON ARBORETUM

used as a street tree in Yunnan where it is native and I have seen it growing in gardens in Hangzhou. *M. lotungensis* is androdioecious and our plant unfortunately has strictly male flowers.

Nearby in our Asian Valley, from section Gwillimia is a pink flowered form of *M. delavayi*. This has made a somewhat shrubby plant with bold foliage and stout stems. Most plants I have seen are rather coarse in all seasons. The large foliage to 35cm has silvery backs and a ruffled leaf surface. Huge, fleshy buds give rise to 25cm flowers which are typically blush white. The JCRA plant is a pink form which has been passed around horticultural circles. Unfortu-nately the colour is somewhat fleshy and tends to resemble a typical white magnolia flower which has been nipped by frost. Our plant has taken some winter damage but has still flowered well. When temperatures drop to around -7°C, the foliage is often damaged and begins to drop. At -13°C or when temperatures stay below 0°C for several days, there can be fairly significant stem damage.

Another mostly evergreen section, Manglietia, is home to *M. fordiana* a lovely, very upright evergreen tree which has been much confused in the U.S. trade with the hardier *M. yuyuanensis*. Both make beautiful specimens but can be painfully slow to flower and difficult to propagate. A hedge of the latter was planted at the JCRA

with the intention of coppicing in the hopes that the young, vigorous, pseudojuvenile shoots would root more readily but to date we have balked at the seeming sacrilege when confronting them with the pruning saw. Perhaps the most beloved species in this section, at least by JCRA visitors, is *M. kwangtungensis* whose plump flower buds drip from branch tips, opening to downward facing flowers. When this narrowly upright tree is in full flower, standing beneath it gazing up into the flowers is a magical experience.

A remarkably rare member of this section, *M. xinganensis* is proving to be quite hardy. The cup shaped, thick textured flowers bear "horizontally undulate striations" which give the flowers the appearance of crackle glaze pottery. We have only been growing this plant from Guanxi Province for a short while but it looks to be a quite vigorous species. Seed of this species has been sent to Cornwall I understand and will hopefully find its way throughout Europe.

The JCRA of course also has significant collections of deciduous magnolias in section Yulania with a multitude of plants ranging from *M. amoena* to *M. zenii*. We love the delicate pink to white flowers of both species with a darker central zone and purplish anthers in the former, reddish in the latter. The large flowers on bare early spring branches are highlights of the eastern end of the Arboretum along with the bulk of the magnolia collection.

MAGNOLIA KWANGTUNGENSIS
MARK WEATHINGTON & JC RAULSTON ARBORETUM

MAGNOLIA 'CORAL LAKE'
MARK WEATHINGTON & JC RAULSTON ARBORETUM

MAGNOLIA STELLATA
'CHRYSANTHEMUMIFLORA'
MARK WEATHINGTON & JC RAULSTON ARBORETUM

MAGNOLIA FOVEOLATA X *LAEVIFOLIA* CROSS
SHOWING GREAT POTENTIAL
MARK WEATHINGTON & JC RAULSTON ARBORETUM

While we hold significant collections of species magnolias, the cultivars also are well represented at the JCRA. 'Coral Lake' is a particular favourite of visitors with its very late, large, double pink flowers highlighted with streaks of yellow. The color of each flower seems to change depending on the ambient light. It has been thriving at the head of our Scree Garden where its April flowers and upright habit form a colourful sentry. An older selection but still one of my personal favourites is *M. stellata* 'Chrysanthemumiflora'. The clear pink colour of the multitude of tepals (36–40) on a small statured tree are unmistakable and in my mind unsurpassed by any other pink star magnolia. We also appreciate the diversity in our own native evergreen magnolias with 12 taxa of *M. virginiana* and 18 of *M. grandiflora*. The small leaved selections of the former such as 'Perdido' and 'Coosa' add an unusual texture to the magnolia collection and should be more widely grown especially in smaller gardens.

We are evaluating quite a few unnamed selections of advance crosses between various species such as *M. foveolata* × *figo* var. *crassipes*, *M. insignis* × *conifera* var. *chingii*, and (*M. laevifolia* × *M. champaca*) × (*M. laevifolia* × *M. maudiae*) from Kevin Parris of Spartanburg

MAGNOLIA VIRGINIANA 'SATELLITE'
MARK WEATHINGTON & JC RAULSTON ARBORETUM

MAGNOLIA FIGO VAR. *CRASSIPES* 'ROYAL ROBES'
MARK WEATHINGTON & JC RAULSTON ARBORETUM

MAGNOLIA STELLATA 'CHRYSANTHEMUMIFLORA'

MARK WEATHINGTON & JC RAULSTON ARBORETUM

Community College in South Carolina and other breeders. Asian evergreen magnolias are just now entering a period of incredibly exciting breeding potential and we anticipate exciting developments in the near future.

The JC Raulston Arboretum has always endeavoured to increase the diversity of the American landscape through evaluation of plant material, display of novel and superior selections,

MAGNOLIA DENUDATA 'FORREST'S PINK'

MARK WEATHINGTON & JC RAULSTON ARBORETUM

and dissemination of knowledge and plants. Over the last 15 years, the JCRA has distributed thousands of plants to nurserymen, other gardens, and Arboretum members. Among these allotments have been magnolia disseminations in larger numbers including *M. sieboldii, M. figo* 'Port Wine', *M. zenii, M. yuyuanensis, M. chapensis, M. laevifolia* 'Michelle', *M. denudata* 'Forrest's Pink', and *M. insignis* among many others. Hopefully we are creating more magnolia enthusiasts in the process.

We are in the process of evaluating our collection, making systematic removals of plants which no longer fit into our collection priorities and aggressively adding new forms. Our dynamic collection keeps the JCRA fresh and ensures that there is always something new to see on each visit. After all, life is too short for boring plants.

MARK WEATHINGTON

is Director and Curator of the JC Raulston Arboretum. He has travelled extensively searching for new plants to diversify the American landscape and is the author of several books and articles on horticulture

Penjerrick Garden and the Legacy of Samuel Smith

PENJERRICK HOUSE   COURTESY OF THE ARCHIVES AND CORNISH STUDIES SERVICE OF THE CORNWALL RECORDS OFFICE

Some readers may know *Rhododendron* 'Penjerrick', a beautiful old hybrid which found particular favour amongst the founders and early members of the Rhododendron Society. H. D. McLaren, Second Lord Aberconway of Bodnant, thought so highly of it that he wrote, *'if the writer were confined to growing one hybrid Rhododendron he would, without hesitation, grow PENJERRICK.'* [1] A smaller number of readers may even know Penjerrick itself: a shadow of its former glory but still a wild and romantically beautiful garden near Falmouth in Cornwall. Towering American conifers grown from original seed introductions and enormous rhododendron specimens now in their senescence hint at the extensive collection once grown there, whilst contemporary reports published in popular gardening periodicals of the

time are a reminder of the illustrious position which Penjerrick once held as one of the most significant British gardens of the 19th century. The garden's fame waxed and waned over time and by the early 20th century its renown was chiefly for the hybridisation work of a now almost completely forgotten figure in the story of British rhododendron cultivation: Samuel Smith.

Penjerrick was one of a number of gardens created in the 19th century by members of the Fox family; a dynasty of Quaker businessmen who, over time, purchased extensive properties in the area and took a keen interest in the development of grounds and gardens, many of which survive today. The Falmouth branch of the family can be traced back to George Croker Fox who, in 1759, settled in the town before going on to found his shipping agency business, Messrs. G. C. Fox and Company.[2] He built a family home, Bank House, on the waterfront near the original quay in Falmouth, and leased the land behind known as 'The Grove' where his son, also George Croker, would later build the impressive property, Grove Hill. The family expanded and acquired more land around the town, but as time went by, it seems that the urge to get away from the hustle and bustle, and perhaps even the crime and disease associated with a busy port, increased. The country homes and gardens created by the family at this time, such as Glendurgan and Trebah, survive and flourish to this day as popular visitor attractions, but it was the farm of Penjerrick, leased by George Croker Fox in 1762[3] which was to become the most famous. George Croker died at Penjerrick in 1781[4] and the lease passed to his nephew Robert Were Fox. Precise details concerning the ownership of the farm and surrounding land over the coming years is

ROBERT WERE FOX, ANNA MARIA FOX AND ROBERT FOX

unclear, but by 1844 the tithe apportionment showed that the land was jointly owned by George Croker's grandsons, George Croker Fox III (from his first son George Croker II) and Robert Were Fox II (from his second son Robert Were) although the main house continued to be occupied by George and Robert's Aunt Mary until her death in 1839.[5] The purchase of the freehold following her death appears to have been the catalyst for the development of the garden within its modern day boundaries.

Credit for the design and creation of the garden at Penjerrick can, on the whole, be attributed to three main figures: Robert Were Fox II (1789–1877), and two of his three children: his son Robert Barclay Fox (1817–1855) and his daughter Anna Maria Fox (1815–1897). The Quaker tradition of journal keeping was one which was practised by all of Robert Were Fox's children, most significantly by his youngest daughter, Caroline, whose diaries were later published in 1881 and provide a valuable social account of the period. It is the diaries of Robert Barclay Fox, however, that reveal most about the development of the garden.

On March 19th 1837, Robert Barclay wrote, '*Walked two miles before breakfast & to Pennance Point before dinner & to Penjerrick before tea. On my return from the latter my father made me the following proposition, which of course I jumped at like gold, viz. Penjerrick estate (which is now let to Uncle G.C. at £20) together with the cottage & four fields adjacent, the croft & all the orchards at the same rent, with the proviso for him to take one or two of the fields at any time should he want to plant &c. & half the produce of the orchards... This is an object which would suit me best of any I could name.*'[6] Over the following couple of years Robert Barclay appears to have concerned himself mainly with the management of his farm estate. His journal records his taking possession of Penjerrick at the end of September 1837 and the following month contains details of a heated disagreement and eventual departure of an unsatisfactory employee. On October 13th he writes, '*A man called Evans came up in the evening to offer himself as Matthey's successor. I hear a good character of him & I mean to give him a fair trial.*'[7] His faith was repaid and it proved to be the beginning of a long and fruitful association with Thomas Evans as manager of the Penjerrick farm estate. By 1839, Robert Barclay had set up bachelor quarters in the cottage at Penjerrick, whilst the main house continued as a second home for his father. During this period there are frequent records of his involvement with the design of the expanding grounds around the estate and it seems that he was very active in assisting his father in the continued development of the beautiful gardens already known to surround the main house too. On June 24th 1839 he wrote, *'a grand day of havoc at Penjerrick. The new owners, Uncle G.C. & my father, made a day of it, slashing the big trees right & left. We had 7 men with hatchets, ropes and saws, & by evening the lawn looked like a battlefield – heaped with prostrate corpses of trees.'* A couple of days later more trees were felled, with Robert Barclay satisfied that the *'place [was] wondrously improved.'*[8] The following year, father and son set about digging out the ponds and Robert Barclay takes credit for laying out the new sweeping drive. In February 1841 he recorded, *'Spite of deep snow & furious easterly wind, my father and I trudged to Penjerrick & accomplished some very effective grouping and building with the large rocks carried yesterday. The snow enabled us to slide them into their allotted sites with great ease.'*[9] The pair were obviously very 'hands on' in their garden landscaping but they were of course assisted by labourers and, later, professional gardeners.

Mention has already been made of Thomas Evans, Robert Barclay's long term farm manager, and safe to say, friend. Throughout his journal, Robert Barclay makes frequent references to his interactions with 'honest Thomas Evans' as he calls him. It is perhaps only to be expected given his Quaker faith that Robert Barclay, like all members of the Society of Friends, would treat his loyal servant with respect and even a great deal of affection. He writes of spending his 21st birthday celebrations at Penjerrick where *'we all stowed away in Evans's parlour, pretty close work, and attacked the cake built for the occasion, the syllabub, peaches &c. with much satisfaction.'*[10] And each Christmas day after concluding the year's accounts for the farm, he would sit down to a roast beef dinner with the Evans family. His entry for Christmas 1841 is quite revealing; *'Henceforth he [Tom] is to share the profits, in addition to his wages, as the just meed of his zeal and industry. Tom's wages are advanced to 10/-, half his time to be mine & the other half spent in*

the higher and lower gardens.'[11] Not only does this show the value placed on Thomas Evans as an employee but also reveals that whilst the farm was certainly Robert Barclay's venture, the garden was still primarily the domain of his father.

After 1843, mention of Robert Barclay's involvement at Penjerrick becomes less frequent as other business affairs, travel and his marriage to Jane Backhouse in 1844 occupied his attention. The marriage went on to yield five children but was to prove tragically short, as ill health forced Robert Barclay to travel to Egypt in 1855 in the hope that the climate might aid his recovery. He died of tuberculosis at Giza, Cairo, on March 10th of that same year,[12] at the age of 38. More tragically still, only five years later, his wife Jane also passed away leaving the children to the care of their grandfather, Robert Were Fox – by now a widower himself – and their two spinster aunts, Anna Maria and Caroline. The eldest child, Robert, was only ten years old.

Little mention is made of the garden at Penjerrick in the coming years save for a few references in Caroline's journal. We know that by 1861, Thomas Evans' long tenure of service as Estate Manager and gardener had come to a close and that he had been succeeded by his son, also Thomas (1822–1889), who by this time was referred to as the Gardener, having previously been employed by the family as a coachman. Penjerrick had continued as a family country retreat until 1872 when Robert Were Fox retired and made it his permanent residence. Robert Were Fox was perhaps the most famous of his family, both for his horticultural achievements, and more particularly for the numerous scientific papers he published. Elected a Fellow of the Royal Society in 1848, his studies largely centred around innovations in mining (his main business interest), the temperature of the earth and magnetism. He also invented the Dipping Needle compass which was employed by Sir James Clarke Ross in his voyage to the Antarctic Ocean in 1837, which of course included the young naturalist, Joseph Dalton Hooker. His position within the scientific community meant that he frequently entertained important guests, one of which was Captain Fitzroy recently returned from his voyage in *HMS Beagle* with Charles Darwin, who brought with him the gift of a brain coral which can still be seen in the garden at Penjerrick today. Significantly for the garden, Robert Were Fox's position also meant that he was often gifted interesting or untested plants by other horticultural enthusiasts of the day. Frederick Hamilton Davey, in 1897, mentions a few specimens in Robert Were Fox's renowned conifer collection: *Cedrus atlantica*, a gift from Mr Pendarves Vivian, *Athrotaxis doniana* from William Shilson of Tremough, and *Pinus webbiana* from Mr Rashleigh of Menabilly.[13] Writing in 1917, J. G. Millais, the great rhododendron historian of his day, recorded that *'Penjerrick was one of the first places to receive the seeds and young plants of Himalayan Rhododendrons, and all of the first species sent home by Sir Joseph Hooker are represented there by huge bushes or small trees.'*[14] Of course it is well known that only a fraction of gardens which lay claim to possessing plants from original Hooker seed introductions can actually prove the connection, but in light of known correspondence between Robert Were Fox and William Hooker[15], his connection to Joseph Dalton Hooker and, at the very least, his friendship with the Shilsons of Tremough, who are known to have received seed for distribution to selected gardens in Cornwall, it seems likely that Penjerrick's claim can be upheld. Certainly the 1871 account of Henry Mills, Head Gardener at the nearby Enys Estate, which recorded *'a fine plant of Rhododendron falconeri'* between 9 and 12 feet high, as well as *Rhododendron thomsonii*, both of which had flowered the previous season, seems to lend further weight to the claim.[16]

Robert Were Fox's scientific interests and passion for experimentation appear to have influenced the creation of his garden. Many writers over the coming decades wrote at length on the beauty of Penjerrick and its unique setting and micro-climate, but it was in 1864 that interest was first drawn to his pioneering work with exotic plants. An article published in the *Journal of the Royal Institute of Cornwall* contained a list of plants growing at Tresco Abbey Gardens, Grove Hill and Penjerrick, taken from Professor Charles Daubeny's *Lectures on Climate*.[17] The list is extensive and diverse, and certainly portrays a plant collection drawn widely from all corners of the globe. An 1865 visitor to Rosehill, the family's primary residence in Falmouth at the time, recorded that *'Mr Fox has naturalised more than 300 exotic species; he has thus brought together the plants of Australia and New Zealand, the trees of the cold countries and those of hot*

ROBERT WERE FOX
COURTESY OF THE ROYAL CORNWALL POLYTECHNIC SOCIETY

countries, loaded all year round with flowers and fruit; large aloes, not imprisoned in a box or under glass houses, but planted freely in the ground... they grow as if they were at home.'[18]

Following the Henry Mills account of 1871, a number of further articles brought Penjerrick national acclaim. One from 1874 gives a detailed account of Robert Were Fox's famed conifer collection, but it is the description of the house which reveals more about the wonder which must have been experienced by visitors to Penjerrick. The writer describes how, after gaining entry to the house via a small door overgrown with fuchsias, they passed through a long glazed passageway filled with plants, to a drawing room containing all manner of books, microscopes, birds, animals, aquaria and even live tree frogs. They then followed the *'amiable daughter of the house'* (presumably Anna Maria) with pet marmoset in tow, through a subterranean tunnel to a grotto covered in ferns and containing pools of golden carp, then through rooms with cockatoos, weaver-birds, monkeys and green parrots, before finally emerging onto the terrace to *'stop almost spell-bound at the fairy-like scene before us.'*[19]

On the July 25th 1877, Robert Were Fox died at the age of 88. The garden, now seemingly coming into its prime, passed to his sole remaining child, Anna Maria, who, at the age of 61, had spent much of her life residing and gardening at Penjerrick.

VIEW FROM PENJERRICK LAWN   COURTESY OF THE ARCHIVES AND CORNISH STUDIES SERVICE OF THE CORNWALL RECORDS OFFICE

friends will not soon forget.'[21] In the same way she also acts as a connecting link in our story of the garden at Penjerrick, for it was she, who in 1889, employed a young man who was to create the plants which were to characterise the next phase of the garden's development.

On July 27th 1889, Thomas Evans junior, Head Gardener and Steward of Penjerrick, died aged 67. Obviously such a garden would require a talented and proficient successor, as well as a man whose temperament suited that of his devoutly religious employer. To find such a man, it seems that Anna Maria turned to personal recommendation, and in particular that of the nephew that she had helped to raise. Joseph Gurney Fox, the youngest son of Robert Barclay Fox, had been only four years old when his father died. As a young adult, he left Falmouth for Newcastle, and then Eastham in Cheshire, where in 1873 he married Margaret May Just, daughter of the Managing Director of the Pacific Steam Co. By 1881 he was living with his wife and his younger sister Jane, at Eastham Vicarage, next door to the home of a retired merchant, whose household included a young under gardener by the name of Samuel Smith. It's unclear how the relationship between Joseph Gurney and this nineteen year-old gardener developed, but we know that in 1889 Samuel travelled to Cornwall to take up his new position as Head Gardener at Penjerrick.

Born in Eastham on June 1st 1861, to Joseph Smith, an agricultural labourer, and his wife Sarah, Samuel was the third of nine children. Nothing is known of his early life until the 1885 record of his marriage in nearby Allerton, Lancashire, to Sarah Hughes, the daughter of a Welsh Farmer. Parish records continue to give us a glimpse into his life, though, through the reports of the births of his four children, three of whom survived: Mary (1887), Sarah (1890) and Annie Conway (1895). A newspaper report from 1900 gives us a valuable insight to the man and his principles. *'Samuel Smith, of Penjerrick, Budock, summoned in respect of the non-vaccination of a child, said he did not secure an*

Anna Maria had inherited her father's love for both science and horticulture, and she shared his passion for conifers in particular. She was also passionate about art and nature, and contemporary reports credited her with the wild beauty carefully cultivated in the garden; most particularly in the lower gardens known as the 'Wilderness'. She was a familiar figure to most residents of the Falmouth area and was very much part of the fabric of local society. Some years after her death one man said of her, *'I regarded Miss Anna Maria as a sweet evangelical Christian... She organised prayer meetings on Sunday afternoons in one of the Penjerrick cottages, and generally took a personal part in them.'*[20] In fact, Anna Maria organised far more than prayer meetings. In 1832, at the age of just seventeen, Anna Maria and Caroline founded the Cornwall Polytechnic Society, later the Royal Cornwall Polytechnic Society under the patronage of King William IV, for the promotion of sciences, arts and literature. Following a long life characterised by charitable works, her obituary of 1897 stated *'Her life was one of the longest, simplest and most beneficent ever lived by a Cornish woman. By her death Falmouth in particular and Cornwall generally have lost a friend whose memory will long be fragrant. She was the connecting link between the past and present generation, and Penjerrick was a rich centre which her many*

ANNA MARIA FOX
COURTESY OF THE ROYAL CORNWALL POLYTECHNIC SOCIETY

tion of vegetables.[24] A few years later, and on the larger stage of the Royal Cornwall Agricultural Show, he won multiple prizes for a diverse range of plants including begonias, ferns, rhododendrons and vegetables.[25] By the time of Anna Maria's death in 1897, glowing reports of the garden were continuing to be published in the national press, and Samuel was even being mentioned by name. One author reported a fine specimen of *Chamaerops excelsa* (now called *Trachycarpus fortunei*) maturing several healthy looking fruit, which he proclaimed as '*a triumph of Mr Smith's, he having last summer tried an experiment in artificial pollination.*'[26] Was this experimentation a precursor for his later work in hybridisation? The celebrated results of Samuel Smith's work as a raiser of rhododendron hybrids came to fruition over the following 30 years, but before we examine in more detail those plants for which he is remembered, let us first consider his work in the context of the day.

The *Rhododendron Society Notes* for 1928 include a fascinating article on Penjerrick Garden, submitted by H. D. McLaren. After discussing Samuel Smith's plants, he praises his success, particularly in light of the fact that '*the raiser of these hybrids had no prior knowledge of the science of heredity, and had necessarily but rare opportunities of visiting other gardens, of discussing his work with other hybridisers, or of obtaining pollen from far afield.*'[27] This could certainly be said to be true when compared to Lord Aberconway and his peers in the Rhododendron Society, but it seems to rather play down the significance of the Cornish horticultural community at the time. As we have already seen, Samuel was a regular exhibitor at local and county shows, and a quick scan through the various lists of exhibitors, winners and judges, reveals the names not only of large estate owners, but also their gardeners: Mr Symons of Carclew, Mr Sangwin of Trelissick, Mr Eddy of Glendurgan, and perhaps most significantly, Mr Gill of Tremough. These were the men with whom Samuel might have discussed his work, and in Richard Gill he would almost certainly have found an inspirational tutor.

Richard Gill was Head Gardener to Henry Shilson at Tremough, near Penryn, and was a pioneer of Indian rhododendron hybridisation. Perhaps most famed for the creation of rhododendrons such as 'Shilsonii' and 'Beauty of Tremough', in later life he founded R. Gill and

exemption order because of ignorance of the law. But was not ignorant of vaccination. Let the law do what it would, he would not have animal matter inserted in his children.'[22] Although this statement was reportedly met with applause, he was still ordered to have his child vaccinated within a fortnight and to pay costs of £1 0s 6d! As a staunch advocate of temperance and a dedicated church-goer, (he was superintendent of Budock Wesleyan Methodist Sunday School for 32 years and laid the foundation stone of Budock Wesleyan Chapel on behalf of the Band of Hope)[23] it is easy to see how, combined with their shared love of horticulture, a close working relationship could have developed between himself and Anna Maria. In Samuel Smith she had found a gardener whose passion for Penjerrick matched her own. He was to work for a further three generations of the family after her death, including Robert Fox, Robert Barclay Fox (or Barclay Fox as he was known), and finally Waldo Trench Fox, before his eventual retirement in 1935.

First mention of Samuel in connection to the garden at Penjerrick comes in an 1890 report on the Royal Cornwall Polytechnic Chrysanthemum Show, where he was awarded a prize for a collec-

Son's Himalayan Nurseries, which became a major supplier of new species and hybrids to the great woodland gardens of the day. In 1888, sometime after the death of his first wife, he was married to Miss M. A. Evans, daughter of Thomas Evans (the younger) of Penjerrick. Although his new father-in-law died within a year of the wedding, it seems likely that Richard would have taken an interest in the garden at Penjerrick, even if only for the sake of his wife who grew up there and his mother-in-law who continued to live near-by for a further nine years. What words of guidance could this experienced head gardener have therefore given to the young Samuel Smith as he began his tenure at Penjerrick? It's amusing to

SAMUEL SMITH   COURTESY OF ANNE WALKER

speculate on the degree to which advice may have been exchanged between these two men, but one thing of which we can be certain is that they did exchange plants. As mentioned, one of Richard Gill's early successes was his 'Beauty of Tremough', a hybrid raised from a blood red form of *Rhododendron arboreum* crossed with *R. griffithianum*. The clone of 'Beauty of Tremough' received a First Class Certificate in 1902 but the remaining seedlings from the cross had been distributed to a select few gardens before they had flowered, and of course one of these gardens was Penjerrick. In April 1904, 'Glory of Penjerrick', with its large blooms showing the influence of *R. griffithianum* but coloured bright carmine, was exhibited for the first time and granted an Award of Merit by the Royal Horticultural Society. Along with 'Shilsonii' it was to go on to feature as a parent in the hybridisation work of Samuel Smith.

Following the death of Anna Maria Fox in 1897, ownership of Penjerrick passed to her nephew Robert Fox (1845–1915), by now a partner in the family shipping agency business and living at Grove Hill in Falmouth. Although records show that Robert Fox continued to support the garden at Penjerrick, and that prizes were awarded for exhibits made in his name, it seems that he was less involved than his aunt and never lived in the house at Penjerrick itself. By 1901 therefore, Samuel and Sarah Smith had become stewards of the estate, living in the main house with their three daughters, and presumably managing the garden with slightly less input from their employer. The relationship between the two families remained strong though. When Robert's son, Barclay was married in February 1900, Samuel and Sarah sent a gift of a silver and glass tea caddy[28], and we know that Samuel later acted as a bearer at Robert Fox's funeral in 1915.[29] It was during this period of relative creative freedom that the majority of Samuel Smith's hybridisation work appears to have been undertaken. One account from 1904 states '*Mr Smith is very keen on hybrid Rhododendrons, and of these he has many thousands in various stages of growth*'.[30] Presumably these 'thousands' may have been the results of relatively few crosses which were later selected or discarded, but even so, given the length of Samuel Smith's career at Penjerrick, it is perhaps a little surprising that he produced only a handful of named varieties. It should of course be pointed out that neither Samuel Smith nor his employers had the money, space or inclination to collect and breed rhododendrons on the scale of gardens such as Caerhays, Bodnant, Exbury or Borde Hill, but it is possible perhaps that this modest rate of production was a creative choice rather than due to limited resources. McClaren attributed a great deal of the success of the planting at Penjerrick to the fact that two thirds of the rhododendrons used were of just five varieties: *Rhododendron arboreum*, 'Barclayi', 'Penjerrick', 'Cornish Cross' and 'Lilianii'. Credit he felt also lay in the fact that '*the head gardener has a keen eye for a good flower, and a ready bonfire for a bad one*'.[31] Whether it was by careful design not to water down the effect or, as McClaren had earlier suggested, it was due to the limited range of plants with which Samuel Smith had to experiment is open to debate, but it is true that records from the period up to Robert Fox's death in 1915 don't include a great number of rhododendron species from which to hybridise.

Although much of Samuel Smith's hybridisation work was carried out during the lifetime of Robert Fox, the plants first flowered and were first exhibited by his son, Robert Barclay Fox (1873–1934). Like his father, Barclay Fox continued to use Grove Hill as his primary address, leaving Samuel and Sarah to run the house at Penjerrick, but records show that he definitely took a keen interest in the garden and was an avid plantsman himself. Fox family archives from the time include correspondence from notable figures such as W. J. Bean, curator of Kew Gardens, Professor Augustine Henry of the College of Science for Ireland, and Frederick Moore of the Royal Botanic Gardens, Glasnevin, as well as garden owners including many of the founding members of the Rhododendron Society. These letters reveal a great deal of trade in new and interesting plants, with requests for propagation material from the garden at Penjerrick being made in return for gifts such as a group of plants sent to Samuel Smith from Kew in 1923, or the first layer of *Rhododendron* 'Loderi Pink Diamond' taken from the plant given to Colonel Stephenson Clark by Sir Edmund Loder. The warmth of these letters sent to Barclay Fox suggest a great deal of respect not only for him and his garden, but also for his head gardener. On the same day that a news-

SAMUEL SMITH IN FRONT OF *PODOCARPUS SALIGNUS* C.1930, STILL AT PENJERRICK AND NOW A UK CHAMPION TREE
PICTURE FROM E. THURSTON'S
TREES AND SHRUBS IN CORNWALL

paper reported the first flowering of Reginald Farrer's introduction of *Rhododendron facetum* at Penjerrick[32], Barclay Fox received a letter from Lionel de Rothschild, obviously in response to an earlier correspondence notifying him of the flower and thanking him for the plant, in which he said '*I am delighted you are pleased with the Facetum… Some day I hope you will come to my garden, or if you cannot manage it you must let your gardener come again in case there are any other seedlings he would like to have. We all owe so much to the glorious rhododendrons which you have produced at Penjerrick that any little thing we can do in return is a great pleasure.*'[33] Whilst great estates such as Exbury were still in their ascendancy and had taken on the baton of rhododendron hybridisation following the huge influx of new Chinese species being introduced, change was unfortunately soon to come to Penjerrick and with it a close to my story of the garden.

ROBERT BARCLAY FOX (*FAR RIGHT*) AND FRIENDS ON THE TERRACE AT PENJERRICK C.1920
COURTESY OF CHARLES FOX

and it proved to be one of his best. The batch was raised at Penjerrick but half of the 400 or so seedlings were given to Richard Gill to grow on, and it was he who named and distributed it more widely. Samuel Smith recalls, '*the name Lilianii was given subsequently by the raiser when one of this cross was shown by him and awarded first prize at Truro in 1911, and he was asked to name it.*'[35] It was shown by Gill at the RHS show the following year where it received an Award of Merit under the name of 'Cornubia'. The form 'Lilianii' which had been shown at Truro, also later received an Award of Merit when it was shown to the RHS by Robert Fox in 1914. Millais and McClaren both report quite some variation across the batch and this is certainly borne out in the surviving plants I have seen at Penjerrick. 'Cornubia' can still be found in larger historic collections although most plants alive today originate from a much smaller genetic stock and are therefore far more consistent. Flowering in March and April, but sometimes earlier, and with a succession of flowers, Millais reports that in a mild year one of his plants flowered continuously for two and a half months! Unfortunately, the original 'Lilianii', a large flowered form named at Penjerrick as 'Naomi', and another form named 'Maeve' all now appear to be lost.

Following the death of Barclay Fox in 1934, and in the absence of any children to pass Penjerrick on to, the estate was left to his nephew Wallace Talbot Trench on the proviso that he adopted the surname Fox, which he duly did, becoming Waldo Trench Fox. The following year, Waldo auctioned much of the contents of the house at Penjerrick before demolishing and rebuilding it. Care of the garden continued under Waldo Fox and his new Head Gardener, Bert Evans, but Samuel and Sarah, now in their mid 70s retired to the village of St Germans, near Plymouth, to live with their daughter Mary and her husband. Sarah died on June 3rd 1939 and Samuel followed her six years later on August 23rd 1945. They are buried together in the old church yard at St Germans.

The following accounts and descriptions include all the known crosses and selections made by Samuel Smith during his long career at Penjerrick. The parentage (in brackets), where known, is given as it appears in the Rhododendron Register.

'Cornubia'

(*arboreum* × 'Shilsonii')
Millais wrote '*If Mr. Smith has raised no other plant we are indebted to him for R. Cornubia.*'[34] Raised around 1901 by crossing a red *Rhododendron arboreum* with 'Shilsonii', itself a cross between *R. barbatum* and *R. thomsonii*, 'Cornubia' was Samuel Smith's first attempt at rhododendron hybridisation,

RHODODENDRON 'CORNUBIA'
NED LOMAX

RHODODENDRON 'TREGEDNA'   COURTESY OF TARANAKI
REGIONAL COUNCIL, NEW ZEALAND

RHODODENDRON 'BARCLAYI'   NED LOMAX

'Tregedna'

(*arboreum* × *thomsonii*)

Smith gives the parentage of this cross as *arboreum* × *thomsonii*,[36] the same as the earlier and perhaps better known 'Harrisii'. However, Millais and McClaren both record it as the reverse cross, with McClaren giving the extra detail that a pink form of *Rhododendron arboreum* acted as the pollen parent. Regardless, 'Tregedna' is now an extremely rare plant. A single specimen survives in the woodland garden at Antony in Cornwall, a gift from Bodnant in 1933, and the only other plant known to the author is at Pukeiti in New Zealand. A very small batch was raised, and by the time of H. D. McClaren's article of 1928, the original plants had already died at Penjerrick. Millais describes the flowers as larger and more brilliant than those of 'Harrisii'.

'Barclayi'

('Glory of Penjerrick' × *thomsonii*)

Raised around the year 1908, *Rhododendron* 'Barclayi' unites the *R. giffithianum* and *R. arboreum* blood of Gill's 'Glory of Penjerrick' with a third Himalayan species, *R. thomsonii*. Millais records that the cross first flowered in 1913 and describes it as a glorified *R. thomsonii*. Several plants were raised and grown on in the garden at Penjerrick, of which five of the best were selected and named. The form 'Robert Fox' A.M. 1921, thought to be the best, was propagated and distributed by the Exeter Veitch nursery and is the most likely to be encountered today. 'Ellen M. Fox', or 'Helen Fox' as it appears in the *Rhododendron Register*, is a form with a deeper crimson flower and was named for Robert Fox's wife. 'Avice', or 'Avis' as it appears in the register, was a larger growing form with paler, unmarked flowers, which along with the forms 'Romala' and 'Waldo' now appear to have been lost. Avice, Romala and Waldo Trench were nieces and nephew to Barclay Fox.

'Werei'

(*arboreum* × *barbatum*)

A chance seedling which was selected from a batch of *Rhododendron arboreum* raised at Penjerrick, 'Werei' was described by Millais as 'the finest rose-pink arboreum' he had ever seen. Very little influence of *R. barbatum* can be seen in the flower although it does show in the leaf and bark. 'Werei' received an Award of Merit in 1921 and although the remaining plant at Penjerrick recently fell over, it survives in collections such as those at Bodnant, Exbury and Windsor Great Park.

'Penjerrick'

(*camplyocarpum* var. *elatum* × *griffithianum*)

Perhaps the best known of all of Samuel Smith's hybrids, 'Penjerrick' is still loved and grown by many rhododendron enthusiasts today. Writing in 1917, Millais records growing this cross (which was yet to flower at that time), indicating that the batch was raised sometime around 1912. No clonal names were ever attributed to these plants and therefore examples of the 'Penjerrick' Group may be encountered in a range of flower colours from ivory-white or pale yellow, through to flushed pink or pure pale pink. The second Lord Aberconway admired these plants so much that he obtained the surplus raised at Penjerrick and planted them as an avenue at Bodnant. This avenue has in recent years been reinstated. 'Penjerrick' received an Award of Merit in 1923. Although the *Rhododendron Register* records *Rhododendron camplyocarpum* var. *elatum* as the seed parent of this cross, Samuel Smith was keen to correct this when writing in 1926, '*the Rho Penjerrick is Griffithianum × Camplyocarpum, and not the reverse as stated in your list.*'[37]

'Cornish Cross'
(*thomsonii × griffithianum*)

In 1924 Millais wrote of 'Cornish Cross', '*by many judges this is considered to be the best new hybrid raised in Cornwall of recent years*'. Although attempted by a number of earlier hybridisers, it is Samuel Smith's cross of *Rhododendron thomsonii* and *R. griffithianum* which proved most successful in its day and

RHODODENDRON 'CORNISH CROSS'   NED LOMAX

has continued to stand the test of time. 'Cornish Cross' was first exhibited at the Falmouth Show of 1923, suggesting that the cross was made slightly earlier than the date of 1920 given by W. J. Bean. It was propagated and distributed by the Veitch nurseries and can still be found in many collections today. Flowers emerge a deep reddish pink and quickly fade to flushed pink. It has perhaps been surpassed by the darker flowered form 'Exbury Cornish Cross' which was later bred from the F.C.C. form of *R. griffithianum* and received an Award of Merit in 1935.

RHODODENDRON 'WEREI'   NED LOMAX

RHODODENDRON 'PENJERRICK'   NED LOMAX

'Budock'

(*thomsonii* × unknown seedling)

McClaren records that the pollen parent for this cross was a deep red hybrid from *Rhododendron griffithianum*, whilst Smith himself records the cross as 'Thomsoni Grandifolia' × 'J.C.W. Seedling',[38] presumably a large-leaved form of *R. thomsonii* crossed with a *R. griffithianum* hybrid obtained from J. C. Williams of Caerhays. McClaren goes on to say that Smith considered 'Budock' to have the best truss of any he had raised and it's certainly true that it is a very handsome plant when in flower. Only a small batch was raised at Penjerrick and it seems that it was not shared with many of the great rhododendron gardens at the time, perhaps due to its very tender nature. Two elderly plants are known to have survived at Glendurgan in the 1980s and, fortunately, propagation material was collected before they both died. 'Budock' is now represented by a single specimen replanted at Glendurgan in the early 1990s.

'Exminster'

(*camplyocarpum* × *thomsonii*)

Raised at Penjerrick but then named and put into commerce by the Veitch nursery at Exeter, 'Exminster' received an Award of Merit in 1923. Smith's own notes give the parentage as 'Thomsoni Grandifolia' × 'Campylocarpum'; the reverse of that given in the register and most likely using the same parent plant as 'Budock'. McClaren records the seed parent as 'thomsonii Grandiflora' which seems more likely as a form collected and distributed by Messers Gill under that name is known to have been in commerce at the time. Described in Gill's catalogue as '*a delightful variety with large bell-shaped flowers, hanging in a laxed truss. The colour varies in shades of apricot, sometimes paling to buff and sulphur pink*', unfortunately 'Exminster' now seems to have been lost.

Two further crosses are recorded in the *Rhododendron Register*. 'Aphrodite', a white *arboreum* × *barbatum* hybrid, shares the same parentage as 'Werei'. 'Glorious' was a cross between an unnamed red hybrid and *Rhododendron thomsonii* and is mentioned by Millais in 1924, most likely seen by him during a visit to Penjerrick two years earlier, although it

RHODODENDRON 'BUDOCK' NED LOMAX

was not mentioned in Smith's 'official' list of 1926. Both crosses now appear to be long since lost. Mention is also made of a few other crosses which were quickly discarded, including 'Lady Alice Fitzwilliam' × *keysii*, which Millais saw in flower at Penjerrick in 1915. He described it as a crinkled form of *R. edgeworthii*, and of a dull bronze-yellow unattractive colour.

I began my research into the life and work of Samuel Smith some years ago and initially it proved difficult to find any information about him, beyond his name listed by a very few authors as the raiser of a number of historic rhododendron cultivars in a small garden in Cornwall. As time went by and I discovered more, I was pleased to find that he did receive recognition for his incredible work during his lifetime. Letters from the Fox family archives show that he was known to, and respected by, the great and the good of the 20th century rhododendron world, with praise for the garden and his work being offered by numerous correspondents and visitors including the great Ernest Wilson. In 1928, he was awarded the Veitch Memorial Medal by the RHS and in 1933 he was even elected an Associate of Honour for his distinguished service to horti-culture, an accolade which was obviously a source of great pride to him and is marked by the inscription on his head stone, Samuel Smith (A.H.). The plants he produced were grown by enthusiasts across the country and were used widely in their own hybridisation work. A quick scan through the *Rhododendron Register* reveals how many new hybrids were raised by the likes of Magor, de Rothschild, Loder and particularly Lord Aberconway, all from Penjerrick plants. Although they never found great commercial success, Smith's plants were offered for sale by nurseries in Britain and as far away as New Zealand. This distribution has meant that, even one hundred or so years after many of them were bred, rhododendrons created by Samuel Smith survive in cultivation today. Some are unfortunately now lost and some only exist as a very few old specimens, but with the assistance of many members of the Rhododendron, Camellia and Magnolia Group, the National Trust Plant Conservation Centre and the micropropagation unit at Duchy College, Rosewarne, I am pleased that most of his plants can be saved and replanted in our gardens for future generations to enjoy. If nothing else, I hope that this article will highlight the importance of the work and legacy of a forgotten figure in the story of rhododendron cultivation, and that maybe a few more of us will remember the name Samuel Smith.

ACKNOWLEDGEMENTS

During the course of writing this article I have received a great deal of help from a wide range of sources. My particular thanks go to Pam Hayward for her assistance in tracking down plants scattered across the country, members of the Rhododendron, Camellia and Magnolia Group for responding to my calls for information, Rachel Morin for allowing me such free access to Penjerrick, its plants and archives, and also to Charles Fox for access to his family photograph albums. I'm very grateful too to Charles Williams for allowing me to use his personal library, to the Cornwall Garden Society for reproducing articles from historic journals for me, and to the descendents of Samuel Smith for their fascinating memories.

REFERENCES

1. H.D. McLaren, *Rhododendron Society Notes 1928,* p. 252
2. Douglas Ellory Pett, *Journal of the Cornwall Garden Society 41, 1998,* p. 91
3. Edgar Thurston, *British and Foreign Trees and Shrubs in Cornwall,* p. 60
4. Douglas Ellory Pett, *ibid*
5. English Heritage, *Register of Historic Parks and Gardens,* 1000513
6. R.L. Brett ed., *Barclay Fox's Journal,* p. 102
7. Ibid, p. 117
8. Ibid, p. 153
9. Ibid, p. 220
10. Ibid, p. 133
11. Ibid, p. 254
12. The Cornish Telegraph, Mining, Agricultural and Commercial Gazette, 11th April 1855
13. F. Hamilton Davey, *West Briton and Cornwall Advertiser, 18th February 1897*
14. J.G. Millais, *Rhododendrons and their Various Hybrids, First Series,* p. 79
15. J. Potter, Lost Gardens, Macmillan 2000, p. 156
16. H. Mills, 1871
17. Jane Bird, *Restoration and Landscape Improvement Plan for Penjerrick Garden,* 3.11
18. J. Potter, Lost Gardens, Macmillan 2000, p. 151
19. The Gardeners' Chronicle, 7th March 1874, p. 308
20. T.J. Porter, *Westcountry Memories of Long Ago, The Western Morning News and Daily Gazette,* 12th August 1938
21. The West Briton and Cornwall Advertiser, 25th November 1897
22. The Cornubian and Redruth Times, 9th November 1900
23. Correspondence from Anne Walker, Great Granddaughter
24. Royal Cornwall Gazette, 20th November 1890
25. The Cornish Telegraph, 21st June 1894
26. F. Hamilton Davey, *ibid*
27. H. D. McClaren, *ibid*, p.252
28. The Leighton Buzzard Observer, 27th February 1900
29. West Briton and Cornwall Advertiser, 13th May 1915
30. The Gardening World, 13th August 1904
31. H. D. McLaren, *ibid,* p. 252
32. The Western Morning News and Mercury, 21st June 1927
33. Lionel de Rothschild, correspondence to R.B. Fox, 21st June 1927
34. J. G. Millais, *ibid,* p. 80
35. ibid
36. ibid
37. ibid
38. ibid

NED LOMAX

is Assistant Head Gardener at The National Trust's Glendurgan Garden, and is a member of the RCMG

The story of *Magnolia globosa* 'White Ensign' and other magnolias growing at Domineys Yard, Dorset

MAGNOLIA GLOBOSA 'WHITE ENSIGN'

WILLIAM GUETERBOCK

We have been making a garden since 1961 and planting an arboretum since 1995 at Domineys Yard, Buckland Newton, Dorset, midway between Dorchester and Sherborne, where the Dorset Downs meet the Blackmore Vale. Now sadly we are selling our house and the neighbouring cottages with the 2.5 acre garden. However, we plan to find a smaller house nearby, and so will be keeping our 2.5 acre arboretum the other side of Locketts Lane, where we have been growing trees and shrubs since 1995, including magnolias, camellias, rhododendrons and azaleas with bulbs, primulas and wild flowers.

The soil is a neutral greensand of varying depths from over thirty feet in the garden to a few inches by the Lydden Stream, which flows through the arboretum. This neutral greensand can be steered towards acidity or alkalinity. Below is clay and gravel with occasional patches of chalk somehow detached from the surrounding Downs. The result is that both plants and weeds thrive and seedlings from trees, shrubs and other plants abound. This makes weeding almost a botanical expedition. The climate is good and cold air drains into the lower ground and the vale beyond. This gives us areas with good microclimates. We now have about 150 camellias in the garden and arboretum and our first rhododendron was planted in the spring of 1975, joined since then by several more. The smaller ones have been planted in the garden and the larger varieties in the arboretum. There are many other interesting trees in the arboretum, which include a wollemi pine, metasequoias, tulip trees, ginkgo seedlings and some interesting oaks.

The old field hedges surrounding many parts of our garden are home to honey fungus to which we have found magnolias very vulnerable, while camellias and rhododendrons seem resistant since we have not lost any of them. Before we had the arboretum, we had some wonderful magnolias in the garden, but they have mostly succumbed to honey fungus except a few that were planted well away from the hedges. We now grow them in the arboretum, where they thrive. *Magnolia denudata* planted in 1963 and *M. wilsonii* both succumbed but flowered profusely in their final year. *M. wilsonii* produced seed which was germinated, one of whose seedlings is in the arboretum flowering regularly. In turn, its seedlings are now planted out or given to other gardeners.

Planted in 2006, *Magnolia* 'Pickard's Ruby' is now about 7ft high and columnar in growth, flowering profusely right through the spring and even into summer and autumn.

In 2003, I obtained a seedling of *Magnolia globosa*, the hardy Indian form, from John Tremlett, when visiting the garden at Bickham House in Devon just outside Exeter. He told me it was the hardiest of this species and would have hanging white flowers in summer. Planted out in our arboretum on the far side of the Lydden Stream, it first flowered from late May to late June in 2009. To my excitement and surprise, the flowers were not pure white but had red stripes on the inside of the petals which were also flushed with pink inside and pure white on the outside. They were particularly attractive when looked up into with the background of their green leaves against a blue summer sky. At the time that I bought it as a small tree, John told me that he had grown it from seed. When it flowered, I emailed him to ask whether he had in fact made a cross and whether he knew the names of the parent plants; he sadly could not recall. I made enquiries through the RHS magazine *The Plantsman* but while it was known he bred magnolias there was no record of any crosses he had made or where the seed might have come from.

I was put in touch with Peter Catt of Liss Forest Nurseries, who kindly said he would graft some trees, and from the material I posted to him, he grafted eight. Soon after he had grafted them, he accidentally fell out of a tree he was pruning and spent some considerable time in hospital and

'WHITE ENSIGN' FLOWERS

WILLIAM GUETERBOCK

then recovering at home. His grafts of my magnolia were in the nursery with labels marked 'William' and while he was laid up, seven were sold! Unfortunately, there is no record of the buyers, so there are seven grafted plants somewhere labelled 'William'. I managed to rescue the one surviving graft, which flowered that year in the arboretum. The next spring Peter Catt grafted eight more plants and we agreed to share them, and he kindly brought four of these down to Domineys, when visiting the West Country. It was most interesting walking round with him.

As we were going on holiday to Devon in the summer of 2017, I contacted Mrs Tremlett, who said that her husband John had grown the plant, but had died the previous year. She reiterated that she did not know where he got the seed since he not only obtained seed of various sorts through the RHS, but also collected seed from any plant that took his fancy, so it could have come from anywhere he had visited. Maybe someone reading this article will remember exchanging magnolia seeds with him in the 2000s. We gave Mrs Tremlett one of our grafted plants for her to grow in the garden at Bickham House and planted the other three here at Domineys in the arboretum where they have all flowered.

I also arranged with Rae Abrams then Head Gardener at Minterne in Dorset that he would micro-propagate the magnolia, so that it could be made more widely available. Unfortunately all the small plants were killed by vine weevil in the tunnel where he was growing them on. If any reader would like to micro-propagate this magnolia, I would be glad to provide the material.

W. J. Bean in his *Trees and Shrubs Hardy in the British Isles* mentions two sources of the plants of *Magnolia globosa* grown in the UK. One introduction was by George Forrest in 1919 from the Yunnan Tibet border. The other found by Dr Watt in Sikkim, flowered in his greenhouse in 1938 and then was planted out in the garden at Trewithen where Bean says there was also one of Forrest's introductions.

I contacted the International Magnolia Society in the United States and they agreed to name my magnolia 'White Ensign'. The name was chosen as I had spent 34 years serving in the Royal Navy and with the white and red colouration, the name seemed appropriate.

We have a number of plants I have grown from the seed from our 'White Ensign' tree, so it will be exciting to see if they have the red/pink markings on the flowers similar to their parent. It is now a question of waiting for them to flower.

Peter Catt, who is retiring, is keeping one of the grafted plants of 'White Ensign' and tells me he will offer one of the remaining plants to the Savill Garden and the other to the Hillier Arboretum.

Noticing *Magnolia* 'White Ensign' in a Magnolias Society's publication, Mr Luc De Jong emailed me from Belgium, where he has a magnolia collection. We agreed to exchange one of his magnolias 'Pink Axelle' for a 'White Ensign'.

MAGNOLIA 'PINK AXELLE'   LUC DE JONG

Last summer one of his staff delivered this plant to Peter Catt and Peter gave him a grafted plant of 'White Ensign' to take back to Belgium. My son brought the 'Pink Axelle' from Hampshire down to Dorset where it will be planted out in our arboretum in the spring of 2019. Mr De Jong sent me a photo of the flower of 'Pink Axelle', which he said is a seedling of *Magnolia globosa*. He also sent a photo of 'Pink Petticoats' belonging to Maurice Foster, which he said was reputed to be a cross between *Magnolia globosa* and *M. wilsonii*. Both have pink colouration on the inside of the flower.

MAGNOLIA 'PINK PETTICOATS'   MAURICE FOSTER

MAGNOLIA 'THE DUDE'   WILLIAM GUETERBOCK

Three years ago I acquired a bare-rooted standard magnolia seedling, 6ft high, which was going to be thrown out of a garden near Tolpuddle, Dorset. The owner, who grew it from seed, was moving house and did not want it. It was said to be a seedling of *Magnolia* 'The Dude', which I understand is *M. sprengeri* 'Diva' crossed with *M. × soulangea* 'Wada's Picture'. I was told that my small tree came from a seed crossed once again with *M.* 'Wada's Picture'. It would eventually grow into a large tree and I thought it would not flower for many years. It was successfully planted out in the paddock in the centre of the arboretum and settled in well, despite being bare rooted. It is now well shaped and some 8ft high. Last May, much to my surprise, it produced flower buds and had a number of flowers. These are upright and pointed, dark purple at the base becoming lighter until they are white at the tip. I intend to consult the International Magnolia Society about the possibility of naming it. Among the trees in the central paddock as well as the 'Big Dude' seedling there is a grafted 'White Ensign' and a seedling from my original tree as well.

There are many other magnolias in the arboretum. Over the bridge on the far side of the Lydden stream is the original *Magnolia* 'White Ensign', which is now about 20ft tall.

This is the brief story of growing magnolias and many other plants over 58 years in mid Dorset, which have given much pleasure to us and to others, as well as how *Magnolia globosa* 'White Ensign' was discovered. We have learnt much from garden visiting, from both the owners and the gardeners and from the gardening societies both local and national. Talking to nurserymen has also been very helpful, and I would make special mention of Charlie Marchant who ran the nursery started by his father near Ferndown in Dorset. He clearly thought a Naval Officer could not be trusted to plant correctly and for many years would only sell me a variety of tree or shrub after I had taken some soil from the planting spot in for him to test on his bench. Making a garden has been a relaxation, where one can forget the concerns of business and the world. It has involved hard work, as well as many mistakes, but lessons are learnt and an ever increasing fund of knowledge acquired. It is gratifying to know that the garden and arboretum have raised over £50,000 for charity, while giving pleasure to the many visitors to the garden for more than thirty years.

CAPTAIN WILLIAM GUETERBOCK RN CBE
has been gardening at Domineys Yard, Dorset for over fifty years and has been Chairman and President of the Dorset Gardens Trust

The Old Contemptibles hold the line: Hardy Hybrids soldier on

'At these repulsive pies, our offended gorges rise.' This is what Reginald Farrer (1880–1920) reportedly thought of Hardy Hybrid rhododendrons in the gardens of his time. It seemed to be a typical example of the eccentric splendour of his writing style but in fact the lines are borrowed from a Gilbert and Sullivan opera (The Grand Duke) and they refer to sausage rolls. This sharpens the gibe still further.

He clearly disliked what he saw as the unrelieved mounded, rounded 'pies' of the Hardy Hybrid rhododendrons reflecting Victorian formality, massed in parks, flanking walks and drives and forming massive beds, temples of gloom in the 'shrubbery', dense with their heavy green foliage and the regimented quality of their symmetrical flower trusses, melting in the June sun. There may also be a whiff of species snobbery.

His mockery reflects an antipathy, shared by a few other 'rhododendronophobes' of the gardening elite at the time, towards a group of plants which had been a staple of British horticulture for decades. By 1860, several hundred Hardy Hybrids had already been named and introduced, almost all by nurserymen, a result of commercially driven patient cross-breeding to produce what Bean describes as 'vegetable artifacts, bred for the market' and all initially from five species.

Reginald Farrer failed to appreciate the virtues of a plant suited to the everyman gardener around the world. All you needed in order to grow them well was an acid soil. The early hardy hybrids are tolerant of exposed conditions of cold and heat anywhere from New South Wales to Nova Scotia, hardy as an old boot.

Later plants, more suited to UK conditions than continental extremes, remain wind resistant and effective in a variety of situations from full sun to woodland shade; most are resistant to disease and they flower in late May and into June bearing many flowered trusses, late enough to avoid the false promises of a fickle spring.

To be fair, the Farrer disdain was probably more a function of the indiscriminate massed use of hardy hybrids at their peak of popularity – shoddy gardening – than of the plants themselves.

The origins of the early hybrids, the basis of the whole group, have already been well rehearsed. They derive from the five pioneer species – firstly, the indestructible *R. ponticum* (1763) – Frederick Street describes a *ponticum* stump used as a chopping block for two years, then discarded into the garden, where it began to grow.

Then the two tough Americans; *R. catawbiense* (1809) from the high 'balds' of the Appalachians, exposed above the tree line where *Quercus rubra* is dwarfed by the altitude to a few feet, and its neighbour *R. maximum* (1736), flowering in late June to July in the high forest and extending as far north as Nova Scotia.

Add in the equally tough and more compact *R. caucasicum* with its crowded trusses and continuity of flower, and you extend choices still further. Although *R. caucasicum* flowers early, in April, some of its hybrids, such as *R.* 'Cunningham's White' and 'Prince Camille de Rohan', wait until early May.

These species established a foundation of hardiness and flowering time which by crossing, selection, and recrossing, allowed the less reliably hardy but colourful *R. arboreum* (1815) to be brought in to extend the range of colours by a quantum amount. *R. arboreum* first flowered in cultivation in 1825. It was a major turning point. Ernest Wilson wrote 'this marked an epoch in the cult of the rhododendron'.

The plants derived from these five species were reliably covered year after year with beautifully presented tall clusters and trusses of shapely flowers in a spectrum of colours to suit

RHODODENDRON 'FASTUOSUM FLORE PLENO' AGM
DAVID MILLAIS

all tastes – pink, white, cream, reds of many hues, purple, mauve and combinations of all these. And for good measure, many came with variously coloured eyes, spots, flares and blotches. This all made for a rich palette offering a wealth of choice.

It Is an extraordinary tribute to the resilience and flower quality of these early hybrids that after the best part of 175 years, some are still awarded the AGM, the highest accolade granted by the RHS. They still compete, give great garden value, and have persisted because of public acknowledgement of this value, the survival of the fittest. Examples include R. 'Cynthia' AGM, a *catawbiense* hybrid (before 1856), a tower of rosy-crimson, a vigorous grow-anywhere rhododendron; 'Lady Clementine Mitford' AGM (1870), a late R. *maximum* hybrid, peach-pink with prominent brownish flare, also received an AM a century after introduction; the even older 'Madame Masson' AGM (1849), a *catawbiense/ponticum* cross, white with a deep yellow blotch; and in 1846, the double mauve R. 'Fastuosum Flore Pleno' AGM (*see above*), with the same parents, raised in Belgium and still widely encountered in today's gardens. The lack of an award is not to reduce the value of others such as 'Mrs R. S. Holford', a salmon-rose with crimson spots, or popular lower growing scarlet-crimson 'Doncaster' (before 1885), an R. *arboreum* hybrid. There are many more, to suit all preferences.

The introduction of R. *griffithianum* from Sikkim in 1848 provided a further major advance for the Hardy Hybrid, at least for those plants that fall within the definition in the UK, if not in more demanding places like New England and deeply wintry parts of central Europe.

The loose, elegant truss of fragrant, slightly frilled large white flowers was a showstopper; but the lack of hardiness and relatively early flowering were major drawbacks. Amateur breeders such as James Henry Mangles (1832–1884) were interested in flower quality, and less concerned about saleable hardiness. As well as pursuing their own programmes, nurserymen took advantage of Mangles' pioneering work, trying to achieve full hardiness and later flowering while retaining the glamour of his hybrids.

Having said that, one of Mangles' hybrids is 'Loder's White' AGM, arguably among the best weather-resistant whites for general planting and one of the finest Hardy Hybrids ever produced in foliage, habit and flower. Interestingly it is one of only two Hardy Hybrids to appear recently in the Group's Top 100 favourites, both white. Surprisingly, the other was the lanky dark-eyed 'Sappho'. Indeed, only about one third of the Top 100 are hybrids of any kind, perhaps to be anticipated from an enthusiastic group of rhododendron cognoscenti!

It was arch hardy hybridist John Waterer who used the R. *griffithianum* influence to hit the jackpot with the iconic 'Pink Pearl'. He introduced it to an admiring public in 1897. This was a second-generation R. *griffithianum* cross, and although only one-quarter of the gene mix, it preserved something of the large shapely flower of the pollen parent in an imposing hardy hybrid truss. Frederick Street equates its impact and status to seminal plants like *Clematis* 'Jackmanii' and *Geranium* 'Paul Crampel'. It was indeed a breakthrough plant at the time, combining the size and splendour of R. *griffithianum* with the work-aday hardiness of the classic Hardy Hybrid. The public loved it; it is still on sale widely today and tough enough to still be going strong after decades of neglect in old untended gardens, often strewn with bramble and skirted with nettles.

RHODODENDRON 'THE HONOURABLE JEAN MARIE DE MONTAGUE' AGM
DAVID MILLAIS

RHODODENDRON 'ALICE' AGM
DAVID MILLAIS

Examples of other excellent plants with *griffithianum* influence in the flower are 'The Honourable Jean Marie de Montague' AGM (*see above*) with frilled bright red flowers, the classy 'Gomer Waterer' AGM, white edged pale pink, and good in any situation including full sun; 'Alice' AGM (*see above*), a large unspotted rosy pink; and 'Mrs William Watson', lower growing and a pretty blush-white with reddish spotting.

Breeders on the continent soon took up the *griffithianum* challenge, and around the turn of the twentieth century and both Endtz and Koster in Boskoop in the Netherlands produced some excellent Hardy Hybrids to rival both the quality of flower and the hardiness of 'Pink Pearl' or indeed in some eyes, to better it in colour and give a more relaxed quality of truss.

Endtz used 'Pink Pearl' as a parent and produced half a dozen similar pinks. Most have now dropped out of favour in the UK except, perhaps, for 'Souvenir de Doctor S. Endtz' (*see below*), more compact than 'Pink Pearl', with pale pink flowers, and deeper spotting. The large-flowered 'Antoon van Welie', one of our favour-ites, is an example of a good plant no longer readily available. None of the Endtz names trip easily off an English tongue, which may be a factor in their falling from favour.

RHODODENDRON 'SOUVENIR DE DOCTOR S ENDTZ'
MAURICE FOSTER

RHODODENDRON 'BETTY WORMALD'
MAURICE FOSTER

RHODODENDRON 'FAGETTER'S FAVOURITE'

DAVID MILLAIS

Koster went back a generation, eschewing 'Pink Pearl' as a parent and using 'George Hardy', a first cross white *griffithianum* hybrid and actually one of 'Pink Pearl's parents. Crossing it with *catawbiense*, he produced inter alia two plants of top quality in 'Mrs Charles Pearson' AGM, a shapely free-flowering white suffused mauve with brown spots, and 'Betty Wormald' (*see facing page*), large bright pink trusses with red buds and arguably the best pink Hardy Hybrid. Both would be stars in any garden.

The other species brought into play with a degree of success was *R. fortunei*. Its influence produced three top class AGM plants: 'Fagetters Favourite' (*see above*), a clean blush pink; the excellent 'James Burchett' (*see next page*), very late, into the second half of June, a shapely white with a mauve edge and a greenish-brown flare, modest habit and very free flowering; and 'Lavender Girl', a strong grow-anywhere plant with attractive pinkish mauve flowers.

R. griersonianum, massively influential in yielding many fastidious woodland hybrids, produced only one that can reasonably be described as a Hardy Hybrid and that is the 'Earl of Donoughmore' (*see right*), a distinctive red funnel-shaped flower with a suggestion of orange and a spreading habit.

In the 1920s, C B van Nes, the Boskoop nurseryman, bought some first generation *griffithianum* hybrids from a breeder in Berlin called Otto Shultz, which were not hardy and

which he crossed with Hardy Hybrids to produce the popular scarlet-red 'Britannia', and other reds such as 'Earl of Athlone' and 'Unknown Warrior'. These flower rather early and need some shade to be at their best.

As plants for an acid soil, anywhere in the country, in any situation, these Hardy Hybrids are outstanding evergreen flowering shrubs, anchoring deciduous flowering companions such as Oyama magnolias, viburnums, deutzias and early roses and providing a solid green backdrop to enhance the blue and pastel flowers of later flowering hydrangeas.

And anyone who has seen venerable cared-for and carefully pruned plants forming trees in old gardens, their sinewy exfoliating mauve or purple trunks reaching up elegantly to support a domed canopy swathed in flower, can also admire the style and form that comes with age.

Except for the old early ironclads, which will take full sun and full exposure anywhere in the world where there are gardens, most of these plants, while they perform perfectly well in the open in the UK, will prefer a little shade during the hottest part of the day, particularly those that flower late, at midsummer. Having said that, they are not plants bred for the woodland but are easy colourful evergreens for the average garden.

RHODODENDRON 'EARL OF DONOUGHMORE'

DAVID MILLAIS

About 160 Hardy Hybrids, including most of the best, can be seen in the collection at Ramster in Surrey, a conservation collection of immense value both for members of the Group and the public at large. It was set up with the cooperation and help of the Group and we owe a huge debt of gratitude to Miranda and Paul Gunn at Ramster, whose generosity, commitment and enthusiasm have made it all possible. Uniquely in this country, this wonderful collection allows gardeners the opportunity of identifying their own unlabelled plants and making informed and confident choices for planting in their own gardens. And in the absence of old stalwarts who knew their Hardy Hybrid rhododendrons intimately and who are no longer with us, it will become an educational beacon for enthusiasts and garden historians in years to come.

RHODODENDRON 'JAMES BURCHETT'   **DAVID MILLAIS**

THE RAMSTER COLLECTION REVIEWED BY MIRANDA GUNN

It is now nearly 20 years since I first started the Ramster Collection of Hardy Hybrids. John Bond, the then Chairman of the RCM Group wanted to expand the number of plant collections that the Group had already established. He was looking for a site where a representative collection of the large old Hardy Hybrids, fast going out of favour with the garden centres, could be preserved. I had just cleared a 3 acre area of scrappy woodland at the end of the garden, with money that had been left to me by my Uncle Ant, who was a very keen gardener. I named the wood after him, Ant Wood, and was wondering what to put in it. A Hardy Hybrid collection on behalf of the Group seemed the ideal solution and in 2000 the first 190 plants arrived, in 84 varieties. These were planted on a never to be forgotten cold and rainy day in the heavy clay soil on the hill, by Wessex Branch members, along with a wide range of companion plants, kindly donated. The collection now totals about 160 different varieties, over 300 plants in all.

The plan was to have a collection of hardy hybrid rhododendrons raised between 1840–1940, mainly by the great British nurseries, but with a good representation from Dutch and Belgian growers. As it turned out, although most of the rhododendrons in Ant Wood meet the recognised criteria for inclusion as Hardy

Hybrids, the collection is a little loose at the edges and there are some plants that might not quite satisfy the purist. A few of the original plants chosen by John Bond from Knaphill Nurseries were not strictly speaking Hardy Hybrids in terms of the usually accepted definition. I suspect he just added in a few of his favourite hybrids. For example, some of the *caucasicum* hybrids dare to flower in April, and a few Slocock hybrids using *campylocarpum* as a first cross parent were smuggled in.

In addition, several turned out to be wrongly named, so there are now unlabelled plants languishing in the wood, awaiting the day that someone might be able to name them. However, as a result of all this, Ant Wood is in flower from April through to June, with the last two weeks of May being the high point and showing a wonderful range of form and colour. On midsummer's day I have 'Midsummer', a *maximum* hybrid from Waterers, still in flower, and the lovely 'James Burchett' (*see above*).

Although 15 of the hybrids sadly had their AGM rescinded in 2012, I have 24 which have kept it. On top of this, over the decades, there are 23 cultivars in the collection that have been awarded a First Class Certificate by the RHS, and a further 55 have gained an Award of Merit, and some have both from different dates. These are awards to plants for exhibition – essentially as a cut flower arrangement in a vase, demonstrating the beauty of the flower.

WHAT IS A HARDY HYBRID?

This is an historical group of plants bred to succeed as flowering shrubs for general garden use anywhere in the country and in any position to suit the garden layout. They conform to the 2012 RHS Hardiness Ratings H6, being hardy throughout the UK and northern Europe. More specifically, they fully conform to the 1969 RHS Rhododendron Handbook definition of 'A' and 'B' class hybrid rhododendrons which is more detailed:

'A' Hardy anywhere in the British Isles and may be planted in full exposure if desired.

'B' Hardy anywhere in the British Isles but requires some shade to obtain the best results.

The shade requirement does not imply any weakness of constitution, but is simply to mitigate the potentially adverse effects of a strong sun on late flowers.

Contemporary definitions do not vary a great deal:

Bean: A group of nursery bred rhododendrons, ... which are very hardy, flower mostly in late May or June, tolerate exposure and full sun and bear firm upright many flowered trusses in a wide range of colouring.

William Watson: To raise plants that were hardy, sturdy and shapely in growth, so when not in flower they were good looking shrubs, whilst the flower heads, to satisfy the requirements of the time, were to be large and full, the flowers holding themselves up, of good substance, the colours pleasing, and most important of all, they were not to expand before June.

Anthony Waterer: A good garden rhododendron should possess the following qualifications – A strong constitution, large firm foliage, a compact and conical flower head not easily injured by wind or rain and flowering in June or later, thus avoiding frost damage.

NB June flowering is mentioned as a character of major importance throughout, but today most Hardy Hybrids flower in May. This may be a function of a recent sequence of earlier, warmer springs.

There is still room for a few more of these 'Golden Oldies' in the wood, and I am now propagating named plants from other collections, with the help of some members of the Group, with the aim of getting decent plants on their own roots. With the improvements in micropropagation this could also be a way forward. The greatest problem in the Collection is suckering from *ponticum* understocks, and there is a need to be ever-vigilant. Turn your back for a moment and the suckers will shoot up, doing their best to convince the unwary gardener they are the real thing. The Ramster Collection is a valuable conservation resource, and a great reference collection. Few of the rhododendrons in it are readily available now; and nothing gives me more pleasure than seeing a visitor triumphantly clutching some faded blooms which they have succeeded in identifying after visiting the Collection.

FINAL COMMENTS BY MAURICE FOSTER

Hardy Hybrid production slowed soon after the turn of the twentieth century. The best have survived through public demand over these many years of social change and gardening fashion, and 25 have been awarded the AGM for garden excellence following the 2012 review; all are a reflection of the contribution they continue to make to the modern garden.

It is encouraging to note that more are now appearing in local garden centres; and most of those mentioned above are in specialist nursery lists. Surely the 'Old Contemptibles' will not just remain an affectionate memory of one of the most auspicious developments in British horticulture, but will go on decorating our gardens and giving us pleasure long into the future.

REFERENCES

WJ Bean, *Trees and Shrubs hardy in the British Isles*, John Murray

Cox and Cox, *Encyclopaedia of Rhododendron hybrids*, Batsford

Salley and Greer, *Rhododendron hybrids*, Batsford

David Leach, *Rhododendrons of the world*, Scribners

Frederick Street, *Rhododendrons*, Cassell

MIRANDA GUNN

was formerly Chair of Wessex Branch of RCMG. Her home Ramster, near Chiddingfold, Surrey has been in her family since 1922 and was laid out by Gauntlett Nurseries in 1900. Her gardens and the Group Hybrid Collection open mid-March to early June: www.ramsterevents.com

MAURICE FOSTER VMH

is a former Chair of the Group and a renowned woody plantsman who has developed an eclectic range of rare plants at his arboretum near Sevenoaks

Wanderings in the Wild – Plant Hunting in East Taiwan

THE HIGH CENTRAL MOUNTAINS OF TAIWAN, WITH MOUNT NANHU TO THE LEFT RISING TO 3,742M   **RAMA LOPEZ-RIVERA**

During 2014 and 2015, I made a series of expeditions deep into Taiwan's mid-level mountains in search of two little known populations of *Rhododendron pachysanthum*, far outside of their lofty 3,742m home on Mt Nanhu in Taiwan's Central Mountains. Aided by my guide and friend, Tsai-ting 'Ttree' He, we trekked through forgotten landscapes that were once a bustling forestry industry, long since re-claimed by nature and packed with both perils and an incredible richness of rhododendron species awaiting the modern plant hunter.

I had first explored the diversity of Taiwansese rhododendrons while criss-crossing the island in 2010 assisted by the Taiwanese Forestry Research Institute (TFRI), where the trip culminated in a partial ascent of Mt Nanhu, to photograph the stun-ning populations of *R. pachysanthum* found there. This trip was written up as 'A Pachysanthum Puzzle,' a joint article authored by the late Mark Flanagan and me, and published in the RCMG Yearbook 2011. In the article, Mark excellently covered the taxonomic understanding of *R. pachysanthum* to date, while I gave an account of my climb up into its colonies in the wild. At the time, the generally accepted view was that *R. morii* (also in Subsection Maculifera), made up the bulk of lower to mid altitude species on Mt Nanhu, followed by a hybrid zone at around 1,600–2,500m between *R. morii* and *R. pachysanthum* where plants shared characteristics in varying amounts from both parents, before forming into pure stands of *R. pachysanthum* above this as far as the upper summit (where I have since found it growing along-side *R. pseudochrysanthum*). 'A Pachysanthum Puzzle' seemed to tie into this way of thinking quite neatly. However, something about the hybrid zone and this peculiar group of species had always fascinated me, and I wanted to explore this zone on subsequent trips to the mountain's upper reaches.

While on a visit to the herbarium at TFRI Headquarters in Taipei during 2013, I decided to have a look through the voucher specimens of *R.*

RHODODENDRONS SHOWING THE INCREASE OF INDUMENTUM AT MID ELEVATIONS ON NANHU BETWEEN 1,500–2,500M
RAMA LOPEZ-RIVERA

pachysanthum, actually treated in Taiwan as a heavily pubescent form of *R. hyperythrum* specific to Mt Nanhu, and lumped in with the more familiar glabrous *R. hyperythrum* we know from cultivation, but both now using the Taiwanese name (Nanhu dujuan = Mt Nanhu Rhododendron) for what in the West would be considered *R. pachysanthum* – confused yet? Along with the familiar specimens of *R. pachysanthum* with their reddish brown indumentum on the lower side of the leaves collected at various altitudes on Mt Nanhu, my attention was immediately caught by a number of samples under the same name, that I'd never been shown before. While these specimens looked much like plants from Mt Nanhu, sharing similar leaf shapes and reddish indumentum on the leaves, the collection sites were

from three separate locations around Hualien County on Taiwan's East coast, some thirty miles South East of the famous mountain. The collection sites were Heping, Mt Lanshan and Mt Chinsui with the specimens being recorded during the early to mid 1980s by a single collector, Mr Sheng You Liu, who I would only meet much later.

Asking around, no one could add anything further to my enquiries or had heard of the locations (a first for me), saying only that Mr Sheng, a professor in the herbarium had retired some years before. Intrigued so much by the specimens, I concluded that the only way forward was to explore these obscure places for myself and see if I could find any living plants. But first I had to find out where these places were – and luckily I knew just the person to call.

STUNNING UNIFORM LANDSCAPES OF *R. PACHYSANTHUM* ABOVE MIDDLE ELEVATIONS ON NANHU
RAMA LOPEZ-RIVERA

R. PACHYSANTHUM FORMING PURE STANDS JUST ABOVE THE HYBRID ZONE ON NANHU
RAMA LOPEZ-RIVERA

R. PACHYSANTHUM GROWING WITH R. PSEUDOCHRYSANTHUM
AT 3,500 M ON MT NANHU   **RAMA LOPEZ-RIVERA**

Tsai-ting 'Ttree' He had first been sent by TFRI to guide me during my 2010 ascent of Mt Nanhu, while she was working for the herbarium in Taipei. Even then she had a near mythical reputation for her abilities as a mountaineer and wilderness guide among the staff. I had quickly warmed to her relaxed, happy go lucky nature as well as our shared passion for hiking and she had often joined me on some of my further trips to Mt Nanhu. Filling her in on the new locations I'd uncovered, she got back to me within a few days saying she knew the locations as having been former logging stations clustered around Hualien City, until the forestry industry had gone into decline and subsequently been completely cut off during a number of severe earthquakes and typhoons during the late 1980s. Now they were only accessible by foot along difficult and extremely hazardous hikes and had only ever been attempted by a select few sports hiking teams. She told me in her relaxed voice "Super dangerous, lots of snakes and leeches – but sounds exciting"...!

THE HEPING TRAIL

By May 2014, Ttree had identified the Heping Logging Road as our first destination to start the search. Saying goodbye to our driver through thick mist after being dropped as close to the old Heping Road as possible, we hoisted on our packs heavy with food, equipment and supplies and set off for five days of gruelling hiking. The plan was to hike for two days along the Heping Road, before veering off to scale a steep summit that would give

us access to a hiking trail used by sports hiking teams, and then drop down into the distant Taroko National Park, for a further three days to reach the highway and return to Hualien City.

The road surrounded by thick coniferous forest was so entirely overgrown with the grass *Miscanthus sinensis* that we had to use our hiking poles to push our way through. Soon, however, with every few steps I needed to stop to flick off leeches wildly wriggling their way up my legs and arms trying to find a place to feed unnoticed. Miserably continuing like this for the rest of the day before setting up camp under tarps to carry out a methodical leech check, heat a meal, and have a damp night's sleep, occasionally being woken to the rumble of distant landslides.

Starting out at dawn, and although still thick with mist, the way quickly cleared of vegetation, looking much like a regular road again if it wasn't for the strewn boulders and rocks scattered along the route. In places the road had simply vanished, having long fallen off the side of the mountain, requiring us to shuffle along small concrete ledges, using the now exposed reinforcement bars as footing or worse still, throwing our packs first before leaping across gaps, with nothing but fathomless thick mist below causing constant rushes of adrenaline – this was swiftly becoming hair-raising stuff.

THE LABEL TO THIS HERBARIUM SPECIMEN SHOWS
COLLECTION SITES AT HEPING, LISTING THE BOTANICAL
NAME AS *R. HYPERYTHRUM*, WHILE THE TAIWANESE
NAME, NANHU RHODODENDRON, ESSENTIALLY MEANS
R. PACHYSANTHUM   **RAMA LOPEZ-RIVERA**

THE HEAVY FOREST AROUND THE HEPING LOGGING ROAD
RAMA LOPEZ-RIVERA

Soon, however, I was overjoyed to see our first rhododendrons along the road sides, some with an attractive brown indumentum on the undersides of the leaves. I was reminded of both the herbarium specimens I'd seen, as well as some sheltered mid-elevation plants on Mt Nanhu, although our altitude was lower at around 1,400m. Soon after, I started to find plants without indumentum, similar to *R. morii*, but otherwise just like those with indumentum. Collecting herbarium samples of these to deposit in the herbarium in Taipei, I was amazed by the incredible richness of rhododendron species in the area, seeing stunning plants of *R. ellipticum* in bloom along with a number of unusual members of Section Tsutsusi; *R. taiwanalpinum*, *R. breviperulatum* and the very pubescent *R. oldhamii*. *Rhododendron formosanum* was also in the area, sharing some strong similarities with the *morii*-type specimens, but overall noticeably different in appearance and uniformity from the former. Pushing on for our final night on the actual Heping Road, we stayed in an old forestry building, enjoying a fantastic meal and a good night's sleep out of the chilly damp mist.

Rising early for the long steep climb away from the road towards our target summit, we reached the 2,200m plateau full of *Rhododendron morii* mixed with varying stages of indumentum and basking in warm midday sun. Being the highest peak in the area, I began contemplating whether this mix of features was due to environmental factors, or if these plants were just genetically unstable, throwing out different features. After a brief rest, we quickly began our final three-day descent along a clear hiking trail into dark dank forest to the distant highway below.

LANSHAN

In October 2015, Ttree and I joined William Chen, another former hiking companion, and set out on the next leg of my search for this peculiar rhododendron. For this journey we had identified Lanshan, a virtually forgotten mountain range south of the Mugua River in Hualien Country, for our primary search area. Like the Heping Logging Road, Lanshan was once a major source of timber production, eventually becoming the largest forestry site in Taiwan, but long since shut down and cut off from the outside world after environmental reforms put an end to the industry. The area had now become extremely wild and hazardous, only ever accessed by indigenous hunters and sports hiking teams. Our journey would start with a near vertical ascent out of a deep river valley for two full days, before reaching Fufushan, an obscure peak giving us access to the spine of the Lanshan Range. This would be followed by dropping first onto a derelict railway built during the Japanese occupation of Taiwan, before a final long descent to our driver a further three days away.

After bidding farewell to our driver at the Tongmen power station by the base of a stunning river valley, we clambered up the edge of a nearby waterfall to begin the long climb. The mountainsides, although heavily vegetated, were beyond steep, quickly requiring us to pull ourselves up using any branches and plants within reach. The problem got alarmingly worse the further we went, as the soft soil beneath each step could only hold weight for two seconds at a time before disintegrating. We were forced to keep climbing, as lingering too long meant having to slam myself arms out against the hillside to stop sliding, or go crashing down to the waterfall now far below.

THE OLD HEPING LOGGING ROAD, STREWN WITH DEBRIS
RAMA LOPEZ-RIVERA

R. ELLIPTICUM ABOVE THE HEPING ROAD

RAMA LOPEZ-RIVERA

R. FORMOSANUM ON HEPING

RAMA LOPEZ-RIVERA

After several hours with only a few breaks on the occasional outcrop of rocks, we reached the plateau making our first camp where I swiftly collapsed into my tent still fully clothed in hiking gear, without eating. The next day, although still, a series of ascents brought a dramatic change in vegetation as we entered dark, humid primeval forest. Everywhere, large ferns were growing at ground level, and clinging to the attractive flaky trunks of huge trees not unlike *Lagerstroemia subcostata* rising high up into the canopy.

Pushing on as best we could, carefully hacking our way through groves of a truly viciously armed little palm, *Calamus quiquesetinervius*. This unusual species has spines running along its stems and leaves, with rope-like tendrils packed with thousands of recurved hooks. These run for many metres through the undergrowth like razor wire and slowed our progress. Finally we reached Fufushan summit, to access our main ridge through the Lanshan range at around 1,700m.

With temperatures starting to fall fast as evening began drawing in, I was feeling an increasing sense of dismay that we hadn't seen any sign of rhododendrons, as our research had suggested we were within the right area and altitude. A little further though, I was met by Ttree, who had been waiting for me by the trail, saying with a knowing grin "Hey Rama, look up!". Above me were large spindly plants not unlike those of *R. pachysanthum* in their leaf shapes, with a thin cinnamon brown indumentum beneath. In a second my mood had lifted as I pushed on with renewed purpose, eagerly inspecting plants, before catching up to help set up the night's camp.

The following morning, after setting off at sunrise, we walked in single file for several hours through the waist height bamboo, *Sasa niitakayamensis*, which now cloaked the ridgeline under the thinning canopy. Taking a short break while Ttree worked out her bearings on the maps, William sat down heavily against a dead tree, still

R. TAIWANALPINUM ON HEPING

RAMA LOPEZ-RIVERA

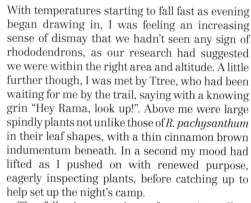

SUMMIT PACKED FULL OF *R. MORII* SHOWING VARIOUS STAGES OF INDUMENTUM

RAMA LOPEZ-RIVERA

TERRAIN TOWARDS LANSHAN   RAMA LOPEZ-RIVERA

carrying his large pack which fell comically sideways. My laughs turned to horror as an orange buzzing cloud of Asian Hornets came swarming out of the fallen trunk. Ttree screamed at us to run as we smashed our way through the undergrowth, scrambling down the steep face of the ridge, all the while trying not to go too close the edge. How none of us were seriously injured or killed, I'll never know, and Ttree skilfully rerouted us, adrenalin pumping, back up to the trail giving the hornets an extremely wide berth!

After a few hours of steady hiking, we reached Mt Qijiaochuan, a high alpine area thick with cloud that marked the highest point of our journey at around 2,400m. Gone were the forests, now with only scattered trees of *Pinus taiwanensis* and *Juniperus chinensis*, but rich in mosses, terrestrial orchids and peculiar alpines that fascinated Ttree and William who seemed to recognise them. Our peculiar rhododendron was popping up again here and there, now more compact with narrower leaves. Soon we were descending fast towards the derelict Lanshan Railway below, reaching the tracks just before nightfall setting up camp surrounded by groves of *Cryptomeria japonica*, planted by the Japanese, filling the air with their scent. Following the old railway the next day we entered an incredible ghost town that was once the thriving Lanshan Work Station complete with houses, offices and even a school, but now completely swallowed up by nature. In 2018, a large multi-agency Taiwanese expedition and film crew fully documented the entire site for a major exhibition in Hualien City, and generously shared a documentary film of the expedition with me.

Continuing into the final part of my own journey, we still occasionally saw our rhododendron along the route, as we walked single file across a number of long rotten bridges crossing deep ravines. Some of these had decayed so badly that just the steel rails were left suspended in mid air forcing me to scoot along on hand and knees, tucking my toes into the edge of the rails and thinking happy thoughts as I saw mossy sleepers and twisted rails far below. I was amazed to watch Ttree walk fearlessly upright the entire time during these sections, turning occasionally to check on our progress, before leading us off for our final long descent back towards civilization and a hot shower!

MT CHIINSUI

Although I was not able to make it to the third site at Mt Chinsui, located just outside Hualien City, Ttree while leading a research group there, kindly took a few tantalizing photos of the most promising rhododendrons, worthy of further investigation. She has very kindly allowed me to include these here.

CONCLUSIONS

Originally named by Bunzo Hayata 1913 as *Rhododendron pachysanthum*, this fine species was then renamed *R. pseudochrysanthum* ssp. *pseudochrysanthum var. rufovelutinum* by Takashi Yamazaki in his 1996 revision of the rhododendrons of Taiwan. The other rhododendrons in subsection Maculifera along with *R. hyperythrum* from subsection Pontica were sunk

HANDSOME RHODODENDRON ON LANSHAN
RAMA LOPEZ-RIVERA

RHODODENDRON IN THE UPPER ALPINE PEAKS OF
LANSHAN   **RAMA LOPEZ-RIVERA**

LOGGING TRAIN LOST IN TIME ON LANSHAN
                                  TSAI-TING HE

into *R. pseudochrysanthum* under various varieties and subspecies, forming a system that is still strictly followed in Japan today. As I mentioned earlier, the Taiwanese system has been revised, with *R. pachysanthum* (Nanhu dujuan) renamed rather than sunk, as *R. hyperythrum*, while what was originally *R. hyperythrum* (Hongshin dujuan) was initially renamed *R. rubropunctatum*, before being sunk into *R. hyperythrum* (Nanhu dujuan), thus making *R. rubropunctatum* defunct. *Rhododendron pseudochrysanthum* (Yushan dujuan), and *R. morii* (Sentsu dujuan) both remain intact, for now, but there are suggestions the whole group should be amalgamated into a single species.

I am not a taxonomist, and it was never my intention to try and unpick the complex naming of the rhododendrons of species Taiwan, but simply to follow a journey that started with my first ascent of Mt Nanhu, and later led me deep into forgotten regions of east Taiwan. I do, however, feel confident that I can on a personal level add a few thoughts to the story. In late 2016, I made the pilgrimage to the prestigious University of Tokyo Herbarium in Japan to view the original type specimens for the rhododendron species of Taiwan. These, along with over a thousand other plant species, were first collected and described during the early 1900s by Bunzo Hayata and his team of collectors, through highly dangerous conditions in the

TRAVERSING THE ABANDONED LANSHAN RAILWAY

                      RAMA LOPEZ-RIVERA AND TSAI-TING HE

STUNNING PLANTS ON MT CHIINSUI

TSAI-TING HE

mountains, where headhunting was still practiced among the island's indigenous peoples until the 1930s. Amongst the university's venerable collection is the type set of *R. pachysanthum* from Mt Nanhu, and collected by Ushinosuke Mori (after whom *R. morii* was named). Seeing these first described specimens was essential to cutting my way through the minefield of nomenclature that surrounds this fascinating rhododendron, and it's close relatives on Taiwan. When viewing Hayata's and Mori's original herbarium specimens of *R. morii* and *R. pachysanthum* in Tokyo that had been collected from Mt Nanhu (along with notes and corrections by Yamazaki), I was pleased to find that they reflected modern samples that I had not only seen in herbariums in Taipei, but also those found on the mountain itself. I was particularly interested in a number that not only resembled the mid-altitude specimens with long narrow leaves and rusty brown indumentum found on Mt Nanhu, but also those collected more recently by Sheng-You Lu on Lanshan, Heping and Mt Chiinsui, who I was delighted to have met in Taipei the previous year.

Reflecting on my own experience in the mountains of Taiwan, and what I've come to know about *R. pachysanthum* in the wild, I believe that it is a form of *R. morii*. In certain situations, altitudes and climatic conditions, *R. morii* begins to form indumentum to varying degrees within sheltered alpine forests, increasing with greater exposure and altitude within these micro-ranges. If mountain peaks in Lanshan, Heping and Mt Chiinsui could reach similar heights to Mt Nanhu's 3742m, we'd have some incredible rhododendrons!

I hope the information about the populations I visited will give Taiwanese researchers additional sources of data for their work on understanding Taiwan's incredible rhododendrons, and I feel extremely privileged to have visited these amazing botanically rich landscapes, so seldom travelled.

ACKNOWLEDGEMENTS

My trips to Heping and Lanshan, would never have been possible without the generous crowd funding support of individuals through Indiegogo.com. I would also like to thank the following for their support and comments: Pam Hayward, Tony Dede & Ann Ridge, Yuji Kurashige, Kenneth Cox, Steve Hootman, Prof. Fuh-Jiuun Pan, Dr Li-Ping Ju, Prof. Yeachen Liu, Prof. Ho-Yih Liu, Prof. Sheng You Liu, William Chen, Dr Shih Wen Chung, Hualien Forest District Office, Vision Way Productions, Prof. Nobuo Kobayashi, David Millais, TAIF, TFRI, Dr Tetsuo Ohi-Toma of Tokyo University for allowing me to view Bunzo Hayata's precious type specimens from Mt Nanhu. Most of all I wish to thank Tsai-ting 'Ttree' He, for always guiding me safely through Taiwan's incredible mountains.

RAMA LOPEZ-RIVERA
is a plantsman and regular traveller to East Asia to see woody plants in the wild. He is also the International Branch Chairman of the RCMG, representing and supporting our overseas members

Rhododendron triumphans Yersin & Chey: an exciting new record for the flora of Laos

CLOSE-UP OF THE FLOWERS

LEAFY BRANCH

Rhododendron triumphans was first collected in Viet Nam on 15th September 1918 by the French botanist and explorer August Chevalier while he was General Inspector of Agriculture and Forests in Indo China (Steenis-Kruseman 1950). It was named by the authors for the beauty of the flowers and the date when it was seen flowering on which they received good news about the war in Europe – what precisely that good news was is not recorded as 'The Great War' had still almost two months to run. It was reported by the collector to be 'a magnificent ornamental plant, remarkable for the beauty of its flowers'.

This species has remained a rarity with no further collections outside its original location from Khánh Hòa (Diên Khánh) on the Massif du Honba, (12° 15′N 109° 06′E). It was recently reported by Romana Rybkova and Vlastik Rybka on a visit to the type locality who observed that it was always growing as an epiphyte in tall forest. There have been reports of this species being sold in the markets in Vietnam but these have never been

substantiated. This remarkable species has recently been observed in Laos. The large bright red flowers are like nothing else recorded in the Indochina region and clearly place this as a '*Vireya Rhododendron*'. Of the 12 *Rhododendron* species recorded in the Laos checklist (2007), only two are vireyas and only *R. chevalieri* Dop is one of the large flowered euvireyas and this species has much smaller cream coloured flowers and very much smaller leaves than the present plant. The photographs clearly show nearly all of the diagnostic characters of *Rhododendron triumphans*. The very large broad red flowers, the spiral arrangement of the leaves and the very long petioles to c.30mm long (described as 18–25mm in the type description (1929). Sleumer (1958) considered this species 'practically identical on morphological grounds' to *Rhododendron brookeanum* Low ex Lindl. (*R. javanicum* Blume subsp. *brookeanum* Argent, A. Lamb & Phillipps) from Borneo but noted the 'striking difference' in the length of the petiole. The characters that cannot be seen from the

BRANCH WITH FLOWERS

HABITAT ON FALLEN TREE

photographs alone are the hairy ovary and glabrous style. The habitat and flowering time (September) certainly fit and the location is not so very far distant (c. 400 km). In the '*javanicum*' complex solidly bright red flowers are unusual although they do occur on the island of Bali and in the somewhat similar *Rhododendron cockburnii* (Argent, A. Lamb & Phillipps) Craven in Borneo. The only other widespread species that has red flowers is *Rhododendron longiflorum* Lindl. which occurs in Thailand and Peninsula Malaysia but has not been recorded in Indochina, and in this species the flowers have a slender tube and are quite different in shape.

This find was made by a Hmong gentleman in Sekong Province who had spent most of his life in the jungle. He said he had never seen this flower before, implying that he thought it a rarity. Laos is however an extremely poorly known country for plant collections. Leong-Škorničková & Newman (2015) quote that only 3 collections per 100km² have been made for Laos compared with 14 for Vietnam and 50 for Thailand. The plant photographed was an epiphyte persisting on a large tree, fallen due to an eroding bank in tall, wet montane forest. One additional specimen was spotted about 50m away around 30m high up a tree. Unfortunately no specimens were taken.

REFERENCES

Leong-Škorničková, J. & Newman, M. 2015. *Gingers of Cambodia, Laos and Vietnam*. Singapore Botanic Gardens, National Parks Board. 1-229.

Newman, M, Ketphanh, S. Svengsuksa, B. Thomas, P. Sengsuksa, K. Lamxay, V. Armstrong, K. 2007. A *Checklist of the Vascular Plants of Lao PDR*. 1-394. Royal Botanic Garden Edinburgh.

Steenis-Kruseman M.J. van, 1950 *Malasian Plant Collectors and Collections Flora Malesiana* Ser. 1 vol. 1: 1-639. Noordhoff-Kolff N.V. Djakarta.

GEORGE ARGENT

is a research associate at the Royal Botanic Garden Edinburgh where he has worked on tropical S.E. Asian Ericaceae for over 40 years. He has travelled extensively in S.E. Asia and is author of the monographic work 'Rhododendrons of Subgenus Vireya' in 2006 (revised 2015)

ANDRE SCHUITEMAN

is Research Leader in the Identification and Naming Department at the Royal Botanic Gardens Kew. He has previously worked as a researcher at the National Herbarium of the Netherlands at Leiden University. His main research interest is the systematics and evolution of Orchidaceae, especially those from Indochina and New Guinea

International Camellia Register and Development of a Camellia Cultivar Dictionary

INTRODUCTION

International registration of the names of cultivated plants is of considerable importance in the disciplines of horticulture, agriculture and forestry. *The International Code of Nomenclature for Cultivated Plants* (ICNCP), also known as the Cultivated Plant Code, is a guide to the rules and regulations for naming cultivars and cultivar groups.

In 1962, the International Camellia Society (ICS) was founded, and was then appointed as the International Cultivar Registration Authority for the Genus *Camellia* at the International Horticultural Congress in Brussels. Thanks to the hard work over 60 years by many camellia horticulturists, enthusiasts and scientists, especially by Ralph Philbrick, Thomas Savige, and Neville Haydon.

The ICR proved that, by prior publication, it could strengthen the system of validity prevent further duplication when selecting names for new cultivars, and assist in clearing up some of the confusion that still clings to a few of the old cultivar names.

In the last two years the ICR has been reviewed, based on the latest version of ICNCP, and it was found that some important issues existing in the ICR should be addressed as soon as possible, especially the re-used (duplicate) names in Japanese cultivars.

1. CHANGE ICR FROM WORD FORMAT TO EXCEL FORMAT

In 1993, *The International Camellia Register*, compiled by Thomas J. Savige, was published in two volumes, totalling 2208 pages. In 1997, the 1st Supplement, compiled by Thomas Savige, was published with 386 pages. In 2011, the 2nd Supplement, compiled by Neville Haydon, was published with 472 pages. These 4 books weigh a total of 7.04kg – more than 15lb. The printed books are heavy to carry and take time to search.

In 2000, Malcolm Perry found that the digital record then existing of the ICR could not be transferred directly to a computer. He therefore scanned the ICR with an early form of optical character recognition software (OCR), which required many corrections. Working with these scans from 2002 to 2005, Neville Haydon corrected the OCR version of the ICR, then added the corrections and began formatting data for a Second Supplement using Word files.

In 2008, the ICS Board decided to make the Register available online, free of charge. Prof. Gianmario Motta of Pavia University, Italy, supervised this project and continues to do so. In December 2009, the Web Camellia Register (WCR) was established and made available from the ICS website.

Unfortunately using the WCR has several disadvantages:

1. there are only 22,374 cultivars names that can be found by searching in the WCR; a search will not find synonyms, orthographic errors, and other departures from accepted names. But those names – including synonyms etc. – are very important for users to search. According to Article 30.1 in the ICNCP, the epithet of a cultivar or group must not be re-used within the same denomination class (for example the genus *Camellia*) for any other cultivar or group. Article 30.1 indicates that if a cultivar name has been used before, whether it is an accepted name or not, that name cannot be reused again. So, besides the accepted names (shown in bold face in the ICR), the WCR should easily make available invalid names as well, including synonyms, different spellings, abbreviations, orthographic errors and other variants, tentative designations, corruptions of the Japanese name, erroneous synonyms, Latin errors, and so on, as listed in the paper ICR.

THE WEB CAMELLIA REGISTER

ZHONGLANG WANG

names, all of which will be published in the third supplement planned for publication in 2020.

So far, the ICR has 23,353 accepted names, most of them (c. 81%) are *C. japonica* and its hybrids (18,917); the second largest category (c. 6.4%) are *C. reticulata* and its hybrids (1492); and the third largest category (c.5.8%) are *C. sasanqua* and its hybrids (1343). In recent years, the number of *C. azalea* hybrids has increased very rapidly to 228 cultivars.

2. The search engine of the WCR is not good enough. If the search strings or words contain non-English characters like in 'Açoreana', 'Zuihôka' or 'Hiryû', the search result will display nothing in the database. Also, sometimes a valid entry may be followed by an invalid entry or by a subset of the description string. This is because some entries include other entries in the printed ICR. The WCR did not include all the entries which it should include, and therefore we felt that it was important that the search engine in WCR should be improved.

In order to manage effectively the ICR and make it easy for people to use it, the ICR in Word form was changed to Excel form, which divides different names in different rows with six columns: Name, Mark, Species or combination, Meaning of oriental names, Believed extinct, and Description, as well as a synonym table of each name in each row with three columns: Name, Description or cited reference, and Accepted name.

Based on the Word files sent by Neville Haydon, after several months' effort and a large number of corrections, all the entries were changed to Excel format. In total, the ICR in four volumes had listed 43,337 cultivar names: 22,021 accepted names, including 3,964 believed extinct or no longer identifiable cultivars, and 21,316 invalid names.

From 2011 to the present, there have been another 1,332 accepted names and 167 invalid

2. THE PROBLEM OF RE-USE OF EPITHETS CAUSING MANY DUPLICATE NAMES

Recently when all the names of cultivars were analysed, a big problem was found with re-used names – duplicate names – which means different cultivars share identical names. According to Article 30.1 and Article 21.22 of the ICNCP, the epithet of a cultivar must not be re-used within the same denomination class (such as the genus *Camellia*) for any other cultivars. Many duplicate names could cause confusion when transliterated or transcribed into Roman characters, especially the names of Japanese cultivars. For example, in the book "Camellias of Japan" (2010) alone, there were 40 names (20 pairs) sharing the same names although they are completely different cultivars. Some of the names are different in Kanji, but when transliterated into Roman characters they are the same. Others are identical both in original Japanese and Roman. This is a very important problem that needed to be solved.

In order to stabilize the names and to comply with the rules in the ICNCP, the decision was made to adopt the following procedure: the first cultivar to bear a name is accepted, while for later-named cultivars, brackets [ ] are used to affix the originator's name, if known, or different species or group, different places of origin, and so on, to distinguish them. In the four books of the ICR, there are 1,982 duplicate names.

Some names have more than two duplicate names, like the name 'Hagoromo' which has 9

CAMELLIA JAPONICA 'HAGOROMO' 1842 (*LEFT*)
CAMELLIA SASANQUA 'HAGOROMO' 1980 (*RIGHT*)

ZHONGLANG WANG

re-used or duplicated names. In addition to re-used identical names, there are 21 names which have the word "hagoromo" as part of a double word name.

3. NAMES WITH THE SAME CHINESE CHARACTERS BOTH IN CHINESE AND IN JAPANESE

In Japanese, there are many Chinese characters called Kanji. Some are identical to Hanzi in Chinese but are pronounced differently. In the ICNCP, there are some articles on how to deal with this. In the future, when new cultivars are published, both in China and in Japan, the instructions in the ICNCP should be followed.

According to Article 21.23 of the ICNCP, a name is not established if, on or after 1 January 1996, its cultivar epithet is (a) so similar in its original written form, or (b) so similar or identical in pronunciation, or (c) so similar or identical in spelling when transliterated or transcribed into the Roman characters to an existing epithet in the denomination class to which the cultivar is assigned, that the name might cause confusion.

4. SOME NAMES ON REVERSE TRANSCRIPTION

In the latest version of the ICNCP there is a new Recommendation 34A.2: where the epithet is taken into a non-alphabetic script from another language, the cultivar name may be established in a form which renders that word or phrase into the nonalphabetic script publication, but when rendered in an alphabetic script should be in its original form where known, and not a transcription of the epithet (published in the nonalphabetic script) (see also Recommendation 27D.3).

Consequently, it is recommended that reverse transcription should return words to their

original form, irrespective of the demands of the transcription system used. For example, the Japanese epithet シルクロード for a camellia cultivar, is derived from the non-Japanese phrase "Silk Road" and should be rendered in an English language publication as 'Silk Road' and not 'Shiruku-rōdo' as it would be transcribed.

But in the ICR, when the cultivars of 'Silk Road' are checked, the following two cultivars are found:

'Shiruku rōdo' (Silk Road), (*C. reticulata* hybrid): Large size, pink to deep pink ground, outer petals red, campanulate semi double, arrayed in a whirl form. Late flowering. Originated in Kyôto Prefecture, Japan. A seedling of 'Shot Silk', (Dayinhong) × Kara-nishiki. Named and released by Ryo Nagao

'Silk Road' (*C. reticulata* hybrid): Medium pink, silk-like texture. Medium size, single form. Strong, upright, well branched growth. Flowers early to midseason. {(*C. pitardii* var *yunnanica* × 'Forty-Niner') × [*C. pitardii* var. *yunnanica* × 'Tiny Princess') × 'Tom Knudsen']}. Originated in 2009 by Daniel Charvet, Fort Bragg, Calif., USA.

The former cultivar (1990) should be rendered in an English language publication as 'Silk Road'and not 'Shiruku-rōdo', but in 2011 the cultivar named 'Silk Road' arrived! If we comply with the rules of Recommendation 34A.2 of the ICNCP (9th edition), then we will have duplicated names for different cultivars.

This is a very difficult problem to deal with even after extensive consultation with Dr Alan C. Leslie of the UK and Dr Jin Xiaobai of China – both members of the International Commission for the Nomenclature of Cultivated Plants, an arm of the International Union of Biological Sciences.

It should be noted that during the process of revision of the ICNCP, some members strongly objected to the addition of the new Recommendation 34A.2, which was initially proposed by the Japanese experts.

The contemporary Japanese language does seem to shift very readily between words written in western languages (mainly English) and the same words rendered in Japanese Katakana, and regards both as equivalent or identical (more readily than the Chinese language treating the words of western languages rendered in Chinese characters imitating the original pronunciation). However, the objection was voted down by the majority of members of the ICNCP, and so Recommendation 34A.2 is there in the current Code.

5. DIACRITICAL MARK

Rules in Article 31.4 (7th edition in 2004), and Recommendation 34D.2 (8th edition in 2009 and 9th edition in 2016) of the ICNCP tackle the subject of diacritical marks – used to indicate when a vowel is to be pronounced long in Romanized epithets transcribed from Kanji, Hiragana, or Katakana.

If a diacritical mark is used, then the macron (overscore) is to be used and not the circumflex or any other mark. As an example, the epithet of *Prunus* 'Chōshū-hizakura' is not to be written as 'Chôshû-hizakura'. However, the ICR already uses the circumflex 'Chôshû-hizakura' and not the overscore 'Chōshū-hizakura'! All of these changes still need to be made in the ICR.

6. SOME OTHER RULES IN ICNCP

There are many rules and recommendations in ICNCP, here are some more that could be misleading, which we should know about. Whilst others are new:

• Publication of a name relating to a Register or Checklist published by an International Cultivar Registration Authority – such as the ICS for the genus *Camellia* – that have appeared only in electronic media, can be made nomenclaturally valid by the printing and deposit of two copies in a designated library (Recommendation 25C of the ICNCP).

• To meet compliance with Recommendation 34D.1 of the ICNCP, transcription of Japanese characters (Kanji, Hiragana, and Katakana) into a script employing the Roman alphabet (Romaji) should be by the modified Hepburn system of Romanization as laid out in the ALA-LC Romanization Tables and employed in Kenkyusha's New Japanese-English Dictionary (edition 3 and later).

• Kenkyusha's New Japanese-English Dictionary differs from the basic ALA-LC Romanization Tables in its presentation of transcribed names by using hyphens. This Code follows the presentation of that Dictionary and uses hyphens to separate the different word elements. Kenkyūsha's *New Japanese-English Dictionary* has long been the largest and most authoritative Japanese-English dictionary.

• Regarding the length of names, it is recommended that an epithet established in a non-Roman script should consist of no more than 30 characters when transliterated or transcribed.

7. DEVELOPING A DIGITAL CAMELLIA DICTIONARY

As printed, the ICR is now too heavy to carry around and too expensive to produce, as well as difficult to use to search for any particular name. To let as many people as possible use the ICR, it is better to have an off-line e-dictionary for mobile phone, tablet and PC.

The ICS Camellia Registrar has developed the first Camellia Digital Dictionary, which can be used on a mobile phone, tablet and computer, together with descriptions, some of which include photos. They also developed some entries in Japanese (Kanji and Hiragana) and in Chinese (Hanzi) for those who want to check the original Japanese and Chinese names and their descriptions. This dictionary

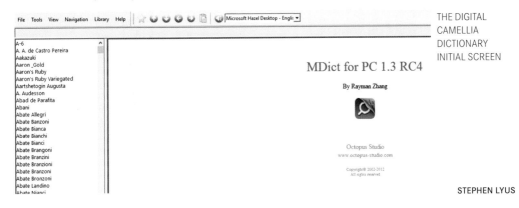

THE DIGITAL CAMELLIA DICTIONARY INITIAL SCREEN

STEPHEN LYUS

supports the HTML language, all blue words in the dictionary could be clicked on to link to the corresponding entry.

Based on software from Octopus Studio, MDict is a dictionary that supports multiple languages. It doesn't come bundled with dictionary data, but its an open platform onto which you can download dictionary data pre-built by others. Key features include:

(a) **Lots of dictionaries.** With an active community, users have made lots of dictionaries. There are over 1,000 databases available in the internet, including Wikipedia.

(b) **Usable on PC, Mobile/cell phones and tablets.** Supports multiple platforms, including Android, IOS and Windows.

(c) **Multiple dictionary lookup.** You can put dictionaries into groups and look up all of them in the same group.

(d) **Pronunciation support.** Supports a true person pronunciation database or TTS engine.

(e) **Clean and friendly user interface (UI).** The UI is clean and friendly, which supports a user in app lookup and cross-app lookup.

(f) **Make and share databases.** MDict provide tools for the ICS to make our own dictionaries and share them with other people. From an Excel file, it is easy to change the format to a Mdict format, and it is easy to use in Android, iOS, and Windows. MDict can also handle photos as will be seen.

INSTALL THE SOFTWARE ON YOUR PC/ TABLET OR PHONE

Please email me (emailslyus@yahoo.co.uk) for the link to get access to the Dropbox folder. In this folder there will be a "Instructions for Dictionary" file, which will describe how to install the software and how to use it.

Spring Formal
[Species or Combination]
C. japonica
[Scientific Name]
Camellia japonica 'Spring Formal'
[Description]
Spring Formal. (C. japonica). ACS., 1986, The Camellia Journal, vol.41, No.3, p.17, Reg. No.2019: A medium sized, deep pink, formal double C.japonica chance seedling of Kumasaka, originated by Nuccio's Nurseries, Altadena, California, USA. American Camellia Yearbook, 1986, p.94: The 15 year old seedling first flowered 1975. Average flower size is 9.5 cm. across. Plant growth is upright, dense and rapid. See colour photo, p.6, International Camellia Journal, No.21, 1989. Chinese synonym: 'Chuntian Yelifu'.

From: book-Jennifer Trehane, 2007. Camellias The Gardener's Encyclopedia

ENTRY FOR *CAMELLIA JAPONICA* 'SPRING FORMAL'   STEPHEN LYUS

ACKNOWLEDGEMENTS

This project was financially supported by the Kunming Institute of Botany: *KIB2016006*, and partly supported by Mr Wu Guichang, Board Chairman of the Palm Landscape Architecture Co. Ltd.

The authors would like to express their sincere thanks to C. D. Brickell (Commission Chairman), A. C. Leslie, and Xiaobai Jin of the International Commission for the Nomenclature of Cultivated Plants for their help on issues of *The International Code of Nomenclature for Cultivated Plants*; and to Prof. Guan Kaiyun, President of the International Camellia Society, Prof. Hu Hong, and Mr Feng Baojun for their help and advice on the work.

Based on Zhonglang Wang's presentation at the 2018 Nantes ICS Conference, modified by Stephen Lyus.

STEPHEN LYUS

retired in 2009 and moved to the Wirral to create a garden for his ericaceous plants. He has been a committee member for many years

Notes from the International Rhododendron Registrar 2018

As many of you will be aware, Alan Leslie, who had been the International Rhododendron Registrar since 1983, retired in June of this year. I replaced Alan as the Registrar at the beginning of August and am happy to be writing what, I hope, will be the first of many Notes from the Registrar.

First, let me briefly introduce myself. My name is Sharon McDonald and I have worked for the Royal Horticultural Society for twelve years as an International Cultivar Registrar. I am the International Registrar for conifers, *Dahlia*, *Dianthus* and *Rhododendron*, having also been the Registrar for daffodils from 2006 to 2013. Previous to the RHS, I worked within the Herbarium at the Royal Botanic Gardens Kew for four and a half years. I am also a member of the executive committee of Hortax – The Cultivated Plant Taxonomy Group: http://www.hortax.org.uk/. My email address is: sharonmcdonald@rhs.org.uk. Any mail should be sent, care of The International Rhododendron Registrar, to: RHS Garden Wisley, Woking, Surrey GU23 6QB, UK.

Registration forms, which have been updated recently due to the EU General Data Protection Regulation (GDPR), are available from me or from our website at: https://www.rhs.org.uk/plants/pdfs/plant-registration-forms/rhododendron-name-registration.PDF

I've tried to follow Alan's format for the Notes, but, at present, I don't have his knowledge or appreciation of rhododendrons, so apologies if they seem a little thin this year. However, I am keen to learn much more about rhododendrons, so that future notes will be more detailed.

At the time of writing we have received 97 registrations, which will be incorporated into the *Fourteenth Supplement to the International Rhododendron Register and Checklist (2004)*, originating from 9 countries. The majority of registrations, this year, are from within Europe (Germany 38, UK 20, France and Latvia 5 each and 1 from Norway), with 26 from the USA and 2 from Australia.

Within those 97 registrations, 26 different species appear in parentages. *R. yakushimanum* (*R. degronianum* ssp. *yakushimanum*) is cited 6 times, with *R. makinoi*, *R. decorum*, *R. hyperythrum* and *R. falconeri* all appearing twice. All of the species, that are listed in parentages this year, have been listed in parentages before, apart from Nearing's form of *R. cinnabarinum* ssp. *xanthocodon*, which is the pollen parent of the lepidote rhododendron '24 Karat' from the USA. The seed parent is *R. keiskei*.

The breakdown of types will not surprise anyone, with 75 elepidotes, 3 lepidotes (no vireyas), 11 evergreen azaleas and 8 deciduous azaleas.

From previous Notes, I'm aware that Alan was enthusiastic about double-flowered rhododendrons, so I'm sure that you will all be glad to know that he was able to register one last double-flowered rhododendron before he retired. 'Mary's House' is a small, evergreen azalea with pale purplish pink, wavy-edged flowers originating from the USA.

Many of the registered names this year are attributed to people, however there are also some names celebrating places or events. For

RHODODENDRON 'MARY'S HOUSE' CLAGETT

RHODODENDRON 'RAF100'   **COLIN MUGRIDGE**

R. 'HACHMANN'S BLACK EYE'   **ODO TSCHETSCH**

example, 'RAF100', with pale flowers, edged with pale purple and with a dark purplish red splotch and spots on the dorsal lobe, is named for the centenary of the UK's Royal Air Force and from Germany, 12 registrations are named for National Parks across the world including 'Malpelo' (*R. yakushimanum* × *R. hyperythrum*), (*see p.102*) with very pale purplish pink flowers, is named for the marine nature reserve in the East Pacific Ocean, 'Masaya' ('Lem's Monarch' × *R. fortunei*), with white and bright pink flowers, named for the Masaya Volcano National Park in Nicaragua and 'Komodo' ('Mariko' × 'Satschiko'), an evergreen azalea, with small bright pink flowers, named for the National Park in Indonesia. Eight of the twelve are evergreen

azaleas, all with 'Mariko' as the seed parent. Pollen parents include 'Blue Danube', 'Satschiko', 'Kermesinum' and 'Madame Albert van Hecke'.

At present, each rhododendron that I receive for registration is a revelation, but I have picked out a few that have particularly caught my eye to describe here. As mentioned previously, these represent inexperienced, personal choices.

The Hachmann nursery in Germany has registered several small rhododendrons, most growing to less than 1m tall in 10 years. Many are highly floriferous and the flowers have strong colours. 'Hachmann's Black Eye' is a good example, having deep reddish purple flowers, with very dark reddish purple spots, overlying bright red-pink blotches on the dorsal

RHODODENDRON 'MASAYA'   **ODO TSCHETSCH**

RHODODENDRON 'KOMODO'   **ODO TSCHETSCH**

RHODODENDRON 'DD GOLD'   HELM

RHODODENDRON 'JOHN ANDERSON'   T. CLARKE

and adjacent lobes. The filaments are pinkish red and the style is bright pink. All very eye-catching!

'DD Gold', from the USA, was the first rhododendron I registered and is really quite striking, with open-faced, tubular funnel-shaped flowers. It is a selection from wild-collected seed of *R. occidentale*. The lobes are very frilled, white, with vivid yellow-orange markings. The dorsal lobe is almost all yellow-orange, whilst the other lobes have stripes of the same colour. The outside of the lobes have touches of pink along the midveins. The long, white slightly curved filaments and style add to the overall pleasing effect.

The flowers of 'Pedro' (*see next page*), a cross between *R. yakushimanum* 'Koichiro Wada' and *R. falconeri* (white form), from Germany, have an understated elegance. They are white, with a blotch of bright pinkish red at the base of the dorsal and adjoining lobes. The lobes are emarginate and it is this which gives the flowers their elegant touch.

'Christine Dohnau' is another of the Hachmann Nursery raisings. Its parentage also includes 'Koichiro Wada' crossed with 'Banderilla' (unregistered). It has pretty campanulate flowers, which are pale yellow, with deeper yellow tones at the base and with a deep pink margin. Full domed trusses sit on small glossy leaves. The plants have grown to 0.65m high in 10 years.

Although less brightly coloured than the above, 'John Anderson' from Exbury Gardens, stands out because of its beautifully shaped ventricose-campanulate flowers. The floriferous conical trusses hold more than 30 pale yellow flowers, each with a dark red blotch at the base of the throat. The white filaments are topped with dark reddish brown anthers and the style and stigma are lemon yellow. The small, multi-stemmed tree has reached 8 × 6m in 20 years.

I'm sure many of you will be aware that Pam Hayward, with help from Alan, has recently produced *The International Rhododendron Register and Checklist (2004) Consolidated*

RHODODENDRON 'CHRISTINE DOHNAU'   ODO TSCHETSCH

RHODODENDRON 'MALPELO'   SCHNUPPER

RHODODENDRON 'PEDRO'   JÄCK

Supplement 2003–2017. This brings together all of the Supplements to the Register up to and including the recently published Thirteenth Supplement. The Consolidated Supplement is available to download from the RCMG website: https://www.rhodogroup-rhs.org/docs/publications/rhodoregister/International%20Rhododendron%20Register%20and%20Checklist%20(2004)%20Consolidated%20Supplement%202003-2017.pdf and the RHS website: https://www.rhs.org.uk/plants/pdfs/plant-register-supplements/Rhododendrons/international-rhodo-consolidated-supplement.pdf. This is a fantastic and very useful piece of work and I am very grateful to all involved for making this happen.

I know that Alan reported on projects that he was working on. One of his big projects, in the last couple of years, was incorporating the names from the Japanese Satsuki Dictionaries into our database. Alan worked his way through around 800 of the entries and I will continue to work on the project with around 500 entries, in the current batch, to add to the Checklist.

On to the administrative side of plant registration. Previously, Alan mentioned that the RHS was working to produce an online registration form. Huge amounts of work, by all of the RHS Registrars and other members of RHS staff, have gone in to the production of the form this year. It has been a complicated and long drawn-out process, but the online Orchid registration form, by far the simplest of the forms, went live earlier this year and has experienced rapid

uptake by registrants (60% is the current rate – to 40% by email or post). The online form for dahlias will go in to its testing phase in the next month or so, with a range of testers, including National Registrars, nursery owners, National Collection holders and individuals from across all of the plant groups for which the RHS is the International Cultivar Registration Authority. Once the dahlia form goes live, the other groups will follow quite quickly. I hope that I will be able to include the address for the rhododendron form in my Notes next year.

The RHS is also in the process of organising a new Horticultural Database, which will incorporate all of our existing plant information databases and give us a much better platform for disseminating our plant name information. This includes being able to provide searchable registration databases online, which we are all very much looking forward to! We are in the early stages, as yet, but there should be some positive news about this next year.

Finally, I would just like to say, please do get in touch with me. I know from my work with the other Registration groups that one of the best ways to learn about a new group of plants is to talk to the people who live and work with those plants. I'm very much looking forward to my first flowering season in 2019 and I'm hoping to meet many of you at shows and competitions next year.

Exceptional Plants 2018
Shows

What is or is not exceptional is bound to be largely a matter of opinion, but there is room for objectivity as well. For example, we can take comfort in the knowledge that the RHS Award of Garden Merit (AGM) is not just an expression of opinion by an unelected elite group, but the result of careful testing of plants against predetermined criteria, though "beauty" and "excellence", however defined, remain at the heart of the judgement. There are also, of course, rules for judging plants exhibited at competitive shows and judges are expected to apply these rules objectively at the same time as exercising their own personal judgment and opinions – a difficult balance to pull off – and it is quite easy for observers to disagree, usually in a respectful way, with the decisions of those judges. All of which brings me to the purpose of this article, which is to give you my own entirely personal selection of plants I have admired at shows and in gardens during 2018.

Some of the plants I mention in these notes are well known and widely grown and, where relevant, I have highlighted cases where the AGM has been awarded because the reader can then be assured that those plants are known to be reliable garden performers and more or less available for purchase. Others are rare and, in some cases, virtually unobtainable for most gardeners. I make no apology for this. Rather, I would prefer it to be seen as positive. Plants tend to become available if there is sufficient demand for them. Our Group is nothing if not a force for conservation of rare plants, and those who are fortunate enough to be the possessors or guardians of exceptional but rare plants are usually generous in providing material for propagation, whether on a small scale for friends or more ambitiously for commercial production.

Every year has its own special character and 2018 was no different. The prolonged heat wave and drought during the summer months created very trying conditions for most of us, but their

RHODODENDRON BARBATUM   **RUSSELL BEESON**

impact is not really going to be seen until 2019. More relevant for the 2018 show and garden visiting season was the sudden bitter weather which descended upon us at the beginning of March. In case anyone has forgotten, the "Beast from the East" collided with storm "Emma", bringing severe sub-zero temperatures and heavy snow falls to many areas, which included many of the most favoured gardens in south west England which normally experience a relatively mild winter and whose horticultural activities are based on that assumption. Severe wind-chill added to the difficulties, creating some of the most damaging conditions experienced in Cornwall and Devon in living memory. Readers in North America or continental Europe may be amused at our British panic when confronted with a bit of snow and ice, but the truth is that it does have an impact when we have become accustomed to gardening on the edge of hardiness expectations.

The impact of the cold weather in March was of course seen most clearly at the early shows in March and early April, though I was really impressed at how successfully most exhibitors had overcome the difficulties they faced.

ROSEMOOR EARLY SPRING SHOW

The biggest problems were those confronting exhibitors at the early spring show at Rosemoor on 10th – 11th March, which included the national Early Camellia and Daffodil Competitions, as well as local competitions for Rhododendrons, Magnolias and Spring Ornamentals, organised by the South West branch with help from RHS staff. Realising that many planned exhibits would have been destroyed by the frost, the organisers thought laterally and greatly simplified the usual classes for rhododendrons and magnolias, and at the same time created new classes for ferns and evergreen shrubs in order to encourage exhibitors to bring along anything and everything of interest in their gardens. This turned out to be an inspired approach which exhibitors embraced with enthusiasm, the result being a colourful and exciting show with a very different look to it.

Rhododendrons and magnolias were hit the hardest by the severe weather only a week or so before the show, even unopened buds being in many cases wiped out. On the other hand camellias, once thought of as tender plants, showed their resilience to the full. While open flowers were frosted, unopened buds rapidly responded to the thaw and most growers were able to gather a good selection of impressive blooms for the show, so the Camellia Competition looked much as it always does and provided the bulk of the colour spectacle of the Show.

Starting with the rhododendrons, which will not detain us long, I noticed some nice early red species, such as **Rhododendron barbatum** exhibited by John Lanyon from Tregye, not perhaps looking quite at its best, but remarkable for being there at all. Apart from these, the few other rhododendron flowers were mainly tender ones of the *Maddenia* and *Vireya* persuasion, which had escaped the worst of the weather by being grown under some protection.

Unsurprisingly, magnolias were largely conspicuous by their absence on this occasion, except to say that Caerhays, in an act of inspired planning, picked some special blooms before the freeze descended and stored them frost-free, so that they could be exhibited in good condition. As well as a fine spray of the very pale purple flowered **Magnolia sargentiana var. robusta** × **sprengeri var. diva**, they also deservedly won

MAGNOLIA SARGENTIANA VAR. *ROBUSTA* X *SPRENGERI* VAR. *DIVA*   **RUSSELL BEESON**

both the Lamellen Cup and the Brother Vincent SSF Cup for a spray and a single bloom respectively of the magnificent and richly coloured **Magnolia 'Bishop Peter'**, which I understand to be a seedling from *Magnolia campbellii* subsp. *mollicomata*.

Camellias were out in force and needed no special consideration in the way that other genera did this year. Marwood Hill and Greenway were probably the most prolific exhibitors

MAGNOLIA 'BISHOP PETER'   **RUSSELL BEESON**

CAMELLIA 'MOUCHANG'　　　RUSSELL BEESON

CAMELLIA 'HAROLD L. PAIGE'　　　RUSSELL BEESON

and one of the most remarkable features of the display was the wide range of cultivars and hybrids of *Camellia reticulata* to be seen. For me, the most impressive blooms were those of '**Mouchang**' and '**Harold L. Paige**', both from Marwood Hill.

The Rosemoor Award for the best camellia bloom in the show went to Marwood Hill for a lovely specimen of ***Camellia japonica* 'Spring Sonnet'**. This semi-double variety from California has pale pink flowers edged with deeper pink and is described as slightly fragrant, though that would have been difficult to detect on a chilly day in March.

It only remains to mention some of the non-RCM exhibits, which made an impressive effect in the hall. As well as *Pieris,* unusual conifers in variety and spectacular displays of evergreen foliage plants such as *Fatsia polycarpa, Schefflera* and mahonias, some unusual and dramatic ferns were to be seen, for example the very rare *Plagiogyria pycnophylla* and a towering ***Lophosoria quadripinnata***, both from Tregye, illustrating the remarkable range of plants grown in the south west and providing wonderful complements to the three genera on which we normally concentrate.

CAMELLIA JAPONICA 'SPRING SONNET'　　RUSSELL BEESON

LOPHOSORIA QUADRIPINNATA　　　RUSSELL BEESON

SAVILL GARDEN, EARLY APRIL

A short report on the Savill Garden show in early April was included in the August 2018 Bulletin, so I will try not to repeat too much of what was said there. The main events were the RHS Early Rhododendron and Main Camellia competitions, but there was plenty to see in the Spring Ornamentals as well – an increasingly well supported part of many of our shows and a demonstration that exhibitors not only achieve wonders with our own three genera but also have much wider interests in a diverse range of trees, shrubs and other plants.

The Crown Estate were not only generous in their hosting of the show but also fully engaged with the event itself, being among the principal exhibitors along with an unusually wide spectrum of large and renowned gardens as well as many enthusiastic amateurs. The result was a spectacular show which the severe weather only a few weeks previously influenced in a benign way by producing a concentration of flowering of both early and mid-season plants. Rather than the same old plants appearing year after year, the vagaries of our weather ensured that we were able to see some rare plants not often seen at our shows.

In the well-supported rhododendron species classes, I noticed **Rhododendron hippophaeoides,** which is a widely grown species of the *Lapponica* sub-section, generally forming a low-growing compact shrub. The most commonly grown form is the excellent 'Haba Shan' AGM clone and this would rightly be most gardeners' first choice for this species. The Crown Estate's specimen under the collectors' number CLDE0515 seemed very distinct to me and equally attractive in its soft

RHODODENDRON HIPPOPHAEOIDES CLDE0515
RUSSELL BEESON

RHODODENDRON THOMSONII VAR. *CANDELABRUM*
RUSSELL BEESON

lavender flowers, beautifully presented on trailing branchlets. I kept coming back to this lovely exhibit, which fully deserved its first prize.

What is one to make of **Rhododendron thomsonii var. candelabrum**? This was the name under which that connoisseur of rhododendron species, Rod White, exhibited a truss which looked very much like the familiar crimson-flowered *R. thomsonii* except in its pink flowers. There is a beautiful illustration of it in *The Rhododendrons of Sikkim-Himalaya* by J. D. Hooker (1849); he called it simply "*R. candelabrum*" but wrote that he now regarded it as just a pale-flowered form of *R. thomsonii*, a species with which he was unfamiliar when he first described the pink form. *Bean* and the 1967 *Rhododendron Handbook* also regarded it as a variety of *R. thomsonii* but by the time the 1998 edition came along it had been relegated to a natural hybrid of *R. thomsonii* and *R. campylocarpum*, so it should strictly be called *Rhododendron × candelabrum*. This is how it is described in other modern publications as well. One might ask: "how do they know?" The answer is that this hybrid (which is quite variable in colour) has been observed in mixed wild populations of the two species, and there seems little doubt as to the plant's true nature. Whatever one calls it, it is a fine looking flower and one that is rarely seen on our show benches. It was exhibited in Class 2 (for species), where it received a 4th prize, so it would appear that the judges were not inclined to be pedantic.

Rhododendrons of the *Vireya* sub-section are making something of a comeback at our shows, which is to be welcomed. A good example was the

RHODODENDRON 'SHOW STOPPER'   RUSSELL BEESON

CAMELLIA 'MIKUNI-NO-HOMARE'   RUSSELL BEESON

vivid red **Rhododendron 'Show Stopper'**, one of two hybrids shown by Exbury, who are building up a fine collection of both hybrid and species vireyas.

The above are just a representative handful of the exceptional rhododendrons seen at this remarkable show. If I mention *R. lanatoides*, *R. tanastylum* and *R. sulfureum* as examples of some of the other rarities on display, the reader may be able to appreciate the riches on view, particularly among the species, which have so often been under-represented at our shows.

As with the Early show at Rosemoor, the bitter early spring weather did not appear to have had much of an impact on the camellias. The benches were laden with magnificent

blooms. The Crown Estate deservedly walked away with the Leonardslee Bowl, awarded for 12 camellia cultivars, but I think it is fitting to illustrate a couple of blooms from the 6 variety class, where Brian and Iris Wright won the South East Branch's Peter Betteley Cup. Firstly, **Camellia 'Arbutus Gum'**, a *C. reticulata × japonica* hybrid, bears elegant semi-double flowers of a rich, clean pink; secondly, **Camellia 'Mikuni-no-homare'**, displays a bright red single flower with a prominent boss of stamens, characteristic of the Higo class of camellias, which are rarely seen in Britain but which have an enthusiastic following in Japan, the USA and Australia in particular. It would be good to see more of these very striking cultivars in our shows.

ROSEMOOR APRIL SPRING SHOW
The central event at the Rosemoor April show is the RHS Main Rhododendron Competition, but there is also plenty of interest in the South West branch Magnolia, Camellia and Floral Display Competitions.

By late April, the cold snap in early spring had largely been forgotten, but its effect was still apparent in the concentration of flowers in late spring, including some which might normally have been expected rather earlier. The recent warm weather, though, had not been sufficient to bring out the 'Loderi' rhododendrons which in many years dominate this show: this year there was not a single one to be seen. Fortunately, there was plenty else to take pleasure in.

Rhododendron niveum AGM is, we are told, not everyone's favourite colour. This does not stop it

CAMELLIA 'ARBUTUS GUM'   RUSSELL BEESON

RHODODENDRON NIVEUM 'CROWN EQUERRY'

RUSSELL BEESON

RHODODENDRON NIVEUM   RUSSELL BEESON

appearing on the show benches regularly and winning prizes more often than not. Perhaps tastes are changing and fewer people take against the very mauve shades. Two distinct forms of the species were on display here. Firstly, a selected clone from the Crown Estate called **Rhododendron niveum 'Crown Equerry'** with flowers at the paler end of the range and, secondly, one simply labelled **Rhododendron niveum** from Trewithen, with a warmer pink colour to it. In their own ways, both were magnificent exhibits displaying full, tight trusses, showing off the species to its best. Trewithen surpassed themselves by also exhibiting a generous spray of the same plant, bearing about 20 trusses. One can only hope that they have not sacrificed too much of their plant in providing us with this spectacle.

R. niveum has passed its colour on to several hybrids, including 'Snowy River', the other parent in this case being the rather similarly coloured *R. ririei*; this excellent free-flowering plant, originally from Bodnant, is popular in the south west but not often seen elsewhere. A perhaps more famous hybrid, this time with *R. falconeri*, is **Rhododendron 'Colonel Rogers'**. An impressive truss of this rather paler coloured flower was shown by the Crown Estate, who won the Loder Challenge Cup for the best hybrid rhododendron in the show.

RHODODENDRON 'COLONEL ROGERS'   RUSSELL BEESON

RHODODENDRON ASTEROCHNOUM   RUSSELL BEESON

Another little-seen species is **Rhododendron asterochnoum**, closely related to *R. calophytum* and bearing pale pink flowers with a pronounced darker blotch. A most striking spray of this species was exhibited by Tregye and was judged to be the best spray in the show, thereby winning the Roza Stevenson Challenge Cup. Few who saw it would disagree.

The *Falconera* sub-section contains a number of species with fine flowers, but most are also noted for their handsome leathery leaves, usually with a pronounced indumentum. A case in point is *R. arizelum*, whose flowers are said to cover a

CAMELLIA JAPONICA 'DESIRE'   RUSSELL BEESON

RHODODENDRON ARIZELUM RUBICOSUM GROUP
RUSSELL BEESON

full range from white, through cream and yellow to pink and crimson. The darker pink forms are often designated as **Rhododendron arizelum Rubicosum Group**, though this exhibit from Caerhays was actually a pale pink with each petal having a darker stripe down the middle. Whatever the name, this was an unusual and very attractive flower.

In the South West Branch Camellia Competition, some fine blooms were on display. The Trewithen Cup is awarded annually for the exhibitor winning the most points and, appropriately enough, it was Trewithen itself which won this trophy, although Marwood Hill and several other competitors gave good accounts of themselves. I have selected two of Trewithen's exhibits for particular mention on this occasion. As it happens, both are cultivars

which have been given the Award of Garden Merit and can therefore be relied upon as first class garden plants. Firstly, **Camellia japonica 'Desire' AGM**, which has a large formal double flower, very full petalled, pale pink edged with deeper pink, making a very impressive exhibit – and I say that as someone who is generally not well-disposed to fully double flowers of any genus. Secondly, **Camellia 'Royalty' AGM**, one of many camellias derived from crosses between forms of *C. japonica* and *C. reticulata*, has large bright pink, semi-double flowers, with the central petals being of a slightly deeper shade and often ruffled.

CAMELLIA 'ROYALTY'   RUSSELL BEESON

Garden visits

GREENWAY, DEVON

In early April, the South West branch visited the beautiful garden at National Trust Greenway, overlooking the Dart estuary in southern Devon. Greenway's most famous attribute is as the home for many years of detective author Agatha Christie. More recently, its garden has become well known for its variety of shrubs and flowers benefitting from the coastal climate, and the quality of its camellias has been recognised by accreditation as a Camellia Garden of Excellence by the International Camellia Society. Of the many camellias seen on this visit I will pick just one, ***Camellia japonica* 'Kimberley'**, not because it is particularly spectacular – in fact the flowers are rather small by the standard of modern cultivars – but because of the exquisitely shaped single scarlet flowers, of a simplicity that has perhaps been lost in more recent developments. This variety probably originated in Japan, but has been in cultivation in Britain certainly since 1900.

THE HILLIER GARDENS, HAMPSHIRE

The Sir Harold Hillier Gardens, near Romsey in Hampshire, have one of the very finest collections of woody plants in Europe, and have had a number of notable curators over the years,

CAMELLIA JAPONICA 'KIMBERLEY'   RUSSELL BEESON

including Roy Lancaster and Jim Gardiner to name but two. Brentry Woodland, just over the road from the main garden, is a delightful area devoted principally to rhododendrons and conifers, but featuring many other outstanding trees and shrubs as well, including a number of fine magnolias. One that caught my eye during April was ***Magnolia* 'Purple Sensation'**, the result of a cross made in New Zealand between *M. liliiflora* and *M. campbellii* subsp. *mollicomata*. This forms an upright but compact small tree, flowering in just 2–4 years as a grafted plant. The pinkish purple flowers have a refined and elegant shape which arguably make it a good substitute for the famous variety 'Lanarth' where a smaller growing tree is required.

RUSSELL BEESON
is an enthusiast for our genera, and also the independent examiner of the Group's accounts

MAGNOLIA 'PURPLE SENSATION'   RUSSELL BEESON

RHS Awards 2018

The Rhododendron, Camellia & Magnolia Group Committee has the privilege of recommending individuals for four prestigious RHS annual awards. The nomination and voting procedure takes place each autumn and the chosen candidates for 2018 have been ratified by the RHS Woody Plant Committee.

THE AJ WALEY MEDAL

Instituted in 1937 by the late Alfred J Waley as an annual award to a working gardener involved with the cultivation of rhododendrons, since 2013 it has been open to any individual engaged in practical or scientific rhododendron matters.

The 2018 Medal recipient is **Harvey Stephens**, a well-known member of the Group. He was trained at RBG Kew and is a former Head Gardener of Borde Hill, where he developed his love for rhododendrons. As Head of the Savill Garden for ten years and Deputy Keeper of the Gardens until recently, he has cared for one of our greatest rhododendron collections. Harvey has promoted genus *Rhododendron* throughout his career, not least in the competitive arena where he has excelled at showing; his attention to detail is legendary As a mentor to junior garden staff, Harvey is inspirational – at Windsor he led and nurtured a happy team who were proud to work for him and learned much; there could be no more appropriate recipient of this award.

HARVEY STEPHENS　　**THE CROWN ESTATE**

CAROLINE BELL　　**CHRISTOPHER BELL**

THE DAVID TREHANE CAMELLIA CUP

Presented to the RHS in 2000 by Miss Jennifer Trehane in memory of her father, David Trehane, it is awarded annually to a person who has significantly promoted or increased knowledge on camellias.

Caroline Bell is a true scholar of genus *Camellia* with an all-consuming passion for camellias on both an intellectual and practical level, a passion she is keen to inspire in others. This can be best appreciated in the in-depth articles contributed to recent editions of the yearbook which reflect the level of her research and her experience of camellia cultivation. At shows and meetings, Caroline is known for the care she takes to bring camellias of interest to educate the public, rather than the glamorous class winners others might choose. Her knowledge of *Camellia sasanqua* is quite extraordinary as is her exceptional know-how on scented varieties and miniatures. The 2018 award recognises her contribution and achievement, and the respect she has attained in the wider camellia community.

CHARLES WILLIAMS vMH

CAERHAYS ESTATE

THE JIM GARDINER MEMORIAL CUP

Awarded for the first time in 2017 in honour of the magnolia enthusiast and Vice President of the RHS, it is awarded annually to a person who has significantly promoted or increased the knowledge of the genus *Magnolia*.

The very word 'magnolia' conjures images of Caerhays in the spring and throughout his adult life **Charles Williams** has sought to maintain and invigorate that effect. Unlike many offspring of gardening giants, Charles has not rested on the laurels of his forebears. Rather, he has conserved devotedly, thoughtfully renewed where necessary, and significantly expanded the collection at Caerhays, pushing boundaries by pursuing a vibrant and imaginative breeding programme as well as sourcing new varieties and trialling borderline species, all to the benefit of the wider magnolia community. He has expounded this passion in written and spoken form: his regular Garden Diary alone demonstrates his commitment to sharing his knowledge of *Magnolia*. Charles is a unique ambassador for magnolias and the 2018 award properly recognises the importance of his enduring contribution.

THE LODER RHODODENDRON CUP

Presented in 1921 by the late Gerald Loder in memory of his brother, Sir Edmund Loder, Bt, this award recognises the value to horticulture of the work of the recipient.

Steve Hootman has been Curator of the Rhododendron Species Botanical Garden in Washington State for over 25 years and Executive Director of the Foundation since 1998. Under his dynamic leadership, the garden has become the centre of rhododendron excellence in cultivation and conservation and now hosts one of the largest living collections of genus *Rhododendron*. He is one of the foremost plant hunters in the world, responsible for introducing many species into culti-

STEVE HOOTMAN

PHILIP EVANS

vation. The internationally acclaimed RSF yearbooks which he initiated in 2006 and the excellent RSF website: www.rhodygarden.org are both examples of his dedication and endeavour. Steve is a true 'giant' in the rhododendron community; highly regarded across the globe, he is a 'go to' person for information, advice and opinion on all matters *Rhododendron*, sharing his unrivalled knowledge with absolute generosity. Steve is a rare beast – a genuine expert in his field with none of those all too familiar 'diva' qualities! The 2018 award represents a perfect recognition of our respect for his on-going contribution to the world of rhododendrons.

Challenge Cups 2018

ALAN HARDY CHALLENGE SALVER

Awarded at the Early Rhododendron Competition to the exhibitor attaining the most points.

The Crown Estate, Windsor Great Park

A SELECTION OF THE EXHIBITS THAT CONTRIBUTED TO THE AWARD (*CLOCKWISE FROM TOP LEFT*):
R. OCHRACEUM COHU 7052;
R. HODGSONII BLM 323;
R. HIPPOPHAEOIDES CLDE 0515;
R. SPINULIFERUM; *R. THOMSONII*
RUSSELL BEESON

THE LIONEL de ROTHSCHILD CHALLENGE CUP

The best exhibit of one truss of each of six species shown in Class 1 of the Main Rhododendron Competition.

Caerhays Castle Gardens

THE WINNING EXHIBIT
RUSSELL BEESON

THE McLAREN CHALLENGE CUP

The best exhibit of any species of rhododendron, one truss shown in Class 3 of the Main Rhododendron Competition.
Trewithen Gardens

Rhododendron falconeri ssp. *falconeri*

RHODODENDRON FALCONERI SSP. FALCONERI   RUSSELL BEESON

THE ROZA STEVENSON CHALLENGE CUP

The best exhibit of any species of rhododendron, one spray or branch with one or more than one truss shown in Class 4 of the Main Rhododendron Competition.
Tregye

Rhododendron asterochnoum

RHODODENDRON ASTEROCHNOUM   RUSSELL BEESON

THE CENTENARY CUP

Awarded at the Harlow Carr Rhododendron Competition to the best exhibit in show.
Ray Wood Volunteers

R. degronianum ssp. *degronianum*

RHODODENDRON DEGRONIANUM SSP. DEGRONIANUM

DAVID MILLAIS

RHODODENDRON 'COLONEL ROGERS' **RUSSELL BEESON**

THE LODER CHALLENGE CUP

The best exhibit of any hybrid rhododendron, one truss shown in Class 34 of the Main Rhododendron Competition.
The Crown Estate, Windsor Great Park

Rhododendron 'Colonel Rogers'

THE CROSFIELD CHALLENGE CUP

The best exhibit of three rhododendrons, raised by or in the garden of the exhibitor, one truss of each shown in Class 36 of the Main Rhododendron Competition (see page 56).
The Crown Estate, Windsor Great Park

R. aberconwayi × *irroratum* (Windsor Hybrid)
R. arboreum × *yakushimanum* (Windsor Hybrid)
R. 'Hope Findlay'

THE WINNING EXHIBIT **RUSSELL BEESON**

THE WINNING EXHIBIT   RUSSELL BEESON

THE LEONARDSLEE BOWL

The best exhibit of twelve cultivars of camellias, one bloom of each shown in Class 10 of the Main Camellia Competition.
The Crown Estate, Windsor Great Park

THE WINNING EXHIBIT   RUSSELL BEESON

THE CHARLES ELEY CENTENARY BOWL

The best exhibit of four trees or shrubs of different genera in bloom, one vase of each.
The Crown Estate, Windsor Great Park

Rhododendron, Camellia & Magnolia Group Trustees & Committee members 2019

Index

RHS GARDEN
Rosemoor

Stunning gardens and amazing events

Including:

RHS National Rhododendron Show
27 & 28 April

Plant Heritage Spring Plant Fair
11 & 12 May

Rose Festival
15 June – 21 July

Rosemoor Garden Flower Show
16 – 18 August

Glow Illuminations
Selected dates November–January

Spring Flower Festival
14 & 15 March 2020

Open every day except Christmas day
Great Torrington, Devon, EX38 8PH
For tickets and promotions visit **rhs.org.uk/rosemoor**
Every visit helps support the charitable work of the RHS

Inspiring everyone to grow

RHS Registered Charity No: 222879/SC038262

CELEBRATING
100 YEARS
EXBURY GARDENS
1919–2019

Exbury
GARDENS
& Steam Railway

Exbury Gardens & Steam Railway is a spectacula[r]
200-acre woodland garden and miniature steam
railway located on the edge of the Beaulieu River

World-famous for the Rothschild collection o[f]
camellias, azaleas and magnolias, Exbury is
celebrating its 100th birthday in 2019. Exbury is als[o]
the birthplace of many rhododendron hybrids, all o[f]
which bloom in a decadent display of colour durin[g]
April and May.

023 8089 1203 | www.exbury.co.uk   New Forest, SO45 1AZ